Shame *and* ANGER:
The Criticism Connection

Brock Hansen, LCSW

www.lulu.com

Change for Good Press
Washington, DC

The painting portrayed on the cover is:

The Broken Window
William Henry Knight
1823–1863

William Henry Knight is best known as a genre painter portraying the moral values of Victorian England. He possessed acute skills of observation and masterfully rendered the details of facial expression, gesture, and costume that capture personality. His favourite subjects were children and his sensitive evocations of the boisterous pastimes of young boys are unsurpassed. *The Broken Window* was chosen for the cover of this book because of its rich portrayal of the postures and facial expressions of criticism, shame, and anger. It is used with permission of Getty Images.

Cover Design by Stewart Andrews

Noodlebox Design, LLC

noodlebox@verizon.net

Library of Congress Catalogue Number   2006909468

ISBN   978-0-6151-3581-6

Dedicated to all my clients, family, and friends
who have been courageous enough
to talk about shame,
but especially to the most thoughtful
contributor to this book,
my dear wife, Penny.

"We are primitive, Dubin.
If we are not to be, we require one another's assistance."
From <u>Ordinary Heroes</u>, by Scott Turow

Author's Note

Criticize This Book!
Please!

The goal of this book is to communicate concepts about shame and anger that will help readers become more confident in the face of criticism and better able to offer criticism with the sensitivity that can make it most effective. Feedback that helps make the book clearer or more complete can make it more successful in this regard. If you have questions or suggestions, I encourage you to make note of them. Where possible, I may be able to clarify some aspect of the book about which you have a question if you email questions and suggestions to me at ShameAndAnger@aol.com. I will do my best to respond directly and will also discuss some of the questions and responses (anonymously to protect your privacy) on my blog at http://shameandanger.blogspot.com.

Some early readers have reported that the book brought them in touch with memories of emotional experiences in their lives or that they recognized current events and their responses to them as colored by emotions which they had not understood in the same way before reading the book. If you have such memories or flashes of recognition, and are willing to share them, I will be glad to add them (anonymously) to the blog. It is my hope that the exchange between the reader and author that is created in this way will expand on the examples and stories I have included in the book and make it clearer and richer.

Thanks in advance for your questions and contributions.

Contents

Section Three
Shame and Anger in the Human Condition

Section One

Our Problems With
Criticism, Shame, and Anger

Chapter One

Introduction

The human infant, though fragile and dependent, comes into the world equipped in many ways for survival. A tiny heart pumps blood to every cell in the body. Tiny lungs take in air, and a little digestive tract is ready to take in nourishment. A baby brain has already begun to learn how to operate muscles and respond to stimuli.

The infant is also born with something that is essential for this small being who will be dependent on others for many years of development and growth: a set of primary emotional responses that have specific survival value. These powerful emotions sometimes seem disproportionately strong for the tiny baby, who can become so overwhelmed by them that parents must rock and cuddle and soothe as best they can to calm the child. But these emotional responses—joy, excitement, distress, fear, shame, anger—are necessary for survival, so the newborn is hardwired with them from birth. She must now begin the long process of learning how to use them in the environment she will soon discover, just as she must learn to use arms and legs and fingers and brain to solve the challenges of life.

This book is about two of these innate emotions—shame and anger—and how and why they dominate our response to criticism by others and by ourselves. It is also about how we can learn to quiet our often painful reactions to the sting of criticism and what we can do to assure that we do not unnecessarily shame others.

As a psychotherapist working for many years with those suffering from depression, addictions, and eating disorders, or those struggling with marital or family conflicts they could not tolerate or solve, I have long been aware of the intense self-criticism and even self-loathing experienced by many of my clients. As a student, I learned various theories of psycho-dynamics that addressed intense self-criticism, but I was not satisfied with any clear and concise terminology for these phenomena until 1990 when I read The Psychology of Shame, by Gershen Kaufman.[1] Dr. Kaufman explores the topic of shame from the point of view of an affect theorist, defining emotions as physiological reactions that include brain activity, release of powerful hormones, and the communicative function of posture and facial expression. He also explores the complex ways in which a shame response can become a learned reaction to various stimuli, and how this can lead to a large number of emotional problems.

Kaufman's clear explanation of the affect of shame rang true for me personally as well as professionally. As the child of a naval officer, moving every two or three years, I regularly experienced the shame of being an outsider in each new school or neighborhood. Like most "new kids," I felt I had to prove myself in the unfamiliar social situation and was sensitive to subtle or blunt signs of rejection. The embarrassment and shyness I experienced were painful for me growing up, but I did not have any explanation for why it felt so uncomfortable. I settled on the belief that I was socially inept, a belief that was reinforced by the emotion of shame and contributed to poor

Introduction

self-esteem that persisted well into adulthood. Kaufman's concepts shed a good deal of light on why I felt this way. I had studied ego psychology, developmental theory, and cognitive therapy and used all of them in my practice, but still found the description of shame as a basic affective state to be unique as an explanation for the power of the embarrassment and shyness that had been my personal trial. The "Aha!" feeling I had upon reading this material was freeing, and I wondered if others would feel the same way about these ideas.

At the time I read Kaufman's book, I was working with a young bulimic woman whose self-image was shockingly distorted. While the world saw her as attractive, kind, and intelligent, she saw herself as ugly and unworthy. Though she understood that others did not see her that way, she could not shake the feeling that her own view of herself was the accurate one. I asked her to draw a picture of the feeling. She drew a simple picture of a round face crying, imprisoned behind the bars of a cage. I thought this picture elegantly expressed the emotion I was reading about in Kaufman's book, and the fact that the emotion of shame is intensified when the shamed individual is exposed to the attention of others like a trapped, caged animal. When I mentioned this to her, she agreed that shame was the perfect term to apply to the emotion that haunted her.

I became interested in the topic of shame and discovered that most of my eating disorder clients could relate instantly to this term. They found the concept of a "shame-based disorder" enlightening, and seemed to feel that this concept helped them to understand themselves and to believe that I understood them better. Many young women with eating disorders (anorexia nervosa and bulimia occur predominantly in women) feel isolated by the fact that most people cannot understand why they seem to despise themselves. Family and friends, and often therapists, try to convince them that they are wrong about the way they perceive themselves. This makes them feel even more deeply misunderstood and confused. Talking about shame as a normal emotion that had become exaggerated and toxic gave them a way to understand the feelings that trapped them and gave us a language that allowed us to explore ways of releasing and resolving these feelings.

I also became interested in another piece of the puzzle, the role that anger plays in shame-based disorders, including addictions and social phobias as well as eating disorders. An individual with a shame-based disorder is ruthless in his self-criticism. The inner dialogue typical of such individuals is characterized by self-directed rage or self-contempt. The angry self-focused diatribe seems to justify and reinforce the shame-based beliefs. But what triggers or precipitates this anger in the first place?

When there has been childhood abuse, we might assume that the victim is angry at the perpetrator but unable to express that anger directly and therefore turns it on herself. This is sometimes the case, but not always. Not all shame-based disorders are the result of childhood abuse and some victims who are clearly able to express anger toward the perpetrator also experience anger at themselves. I became curious about the roots of anger and the relationship between shame and anger.

My curiosity was enhanced by the writings of cognitive therapists like Martin Seligman,[2] and of Daniel Goleman, who writes about the concept of "emotional intelligence."[3] Seligman's books explain in detail how self-defeating thoughts and assumptions become habitual and how cognitive therapy helps with this problem. Goleman not only defines and explores the subject of emotional intelligence, but also introduced me to the field of evolutionary psychology. Evolutionary psychology explores how ancestral environments very different from the one we face today shaped the structure and function of our brains. Fear and anger are clearly explainable in terms of their survival value, but what about shame?

At the same time that I was working with eating disorder clients, I was also seeing clients with addictions, families with parent-child or marital conflicts, and others with workplace issues, depression, or anxiety complaints. I noticed that sensitivity to criticism or overreaction to criticism was a common theme in problematic family and work relationships.

Introduction

Self-criticism or sensitivity to anticipated criticism seemed to be ever present in clients with depression or anxiety complaints, although often it was masked with anger.

Of course it is impossible to interact with others in family, work, or social relationships without encountering criticism. Someone will tell you they don't like something you did, or they don't agree with you on some point or other. When it is important to them, they will probably communicate this with some intensity. And sometimes people are careless about the way they express even casual criticism.

Giving criticism entails making a judgment about whether something or someone is good or bad, better or worse than the critic expects. "This pie is not as good as my grandmother's." "Joe's answers on the history test were incomplete." "Jane was downright rude at your parents' house Saturday night." The critic has a standard in mind and judges the object of his criticism according to that standard. We make so many judgments in everyday life that we quickly become quite confident, even casual about the standards underlying the criticism we give. We may experience little or no emotion when giving criticism. It may seem to us that we are simply stating a fact.

Receiving criticism, however, usually evokes an emotional response. Most of this book is focused on the emotional reactions we have to receiving criticism. Whether the criticism is intended as helpful feedback or a social insult, the recipient is very likely to perceive it as a judgment upon him, triggering the emotional reactions of shame and anger with complex consequences that we will explore in detail.

Almost all of my clients understand intellectually that others have the right to disagree and express their preferences. All of us wish, at times, that others would express their criticism more tactfully. But many clients realize that their personal emotional reactions to receiving criticism are too intense for their own comfort or for effective social interaction. Some grasp the insight that their internal dialogue of self-criticism is terribly exaggerated and cruelly self-punishing, even when they continue to find it difficult to contradict the self-criticism.

Chapter One

It made sense to me that shame and anger were at the heart of this ubiquitous sensitivity to criticism. As I explored these ideas and shared them with my clients in an attempt to help them understand the powerful feelings that compelled them to self-punishing beliefs or dysfunctional reactions to others, many reported that these concepts were helpful. When they asked me for recommended reading, however, I could not find a concise discussion of the relationship between shame and anger in any single book. I was left summarizing the ideas gleaned from several authors, sometimes recommending these sources, and waiting for someone to write the summary my clients were looking for. After awhile, I began to think I would have to write it myself. I wrote a few very brief articles for the lay public and received feedback that these were interesting and helpful ideas. But no single article could quite capture the entire theme, so I have tried to do so in this book.

The book is organized into three sections. In the first, we will explore the evolutionary psychology of the affects of shame and anger, along with its implications for our experience of criticism as individuals and its extreme manifestations in toxic shame and depression. In the second section of the book, we will turn to methods for dealing with the powerful basic emotions of shame and anger so that we are better able to manage harmful reactions to criticism and learn to use the criticism we receive to our advantage. We will then discuss methods for giving criticism without shaming. Finally, we will discuss how to teach children to manage emotional reactions to criticism and explore the many ways in which this is important in the lives of children and families. In the third section, we will detail the significance of shame and anger in our lives beyond the issue of criticism, considering universal aspects of the human condition such as the impact of loss, the ways we deal with shame and anger in society, and the parallels between our discussion of shame and anger and our traditions of spirituality.

The examples I give in an effort to illustrate the concepts I will be discussing are almost all taken from personal or clinical experiences, many shared by clients who bravely told me their

Introduction

stories of shame and anger. These examples are printed in italics and are composites, not intended to describe any specific individual's history. I use the personal pronouns he and she with no special intent to limit any reference to a male or female experience of the emotions or actions described, though I am inclined to use the feminine when discussing eating disorder scenarios.

A word about words

I will use several terms throughout the book that may not be familiar to the general reader but are important concepts for the problems and solutions I will address.

Affect: Although "affect" can be understood as a synonym for emotion in much of this book, affect theorists focus on the physiological manifestations of emotion, our facial expressions and body language. Affect has survival value both in the arousal of the body for action, e.g. the fight-flight response, and in communicating the aroused state to others through posture, facial expression, and other observable behavior. The internal feeling we usually define as emotion is our personal awareness and interpretation of our own affective state. The physical manifestations of affects are hardwired and immediate for survival purposes and occur before we are aware of them as emotions. I will use the term affect throughout this book when I want the reader to be reminded of the physical expression of emotion and its evolutionary significance as distinguished from the internal experience of emotions. Furthermore, because the affective state is primarily a physical behavior, both affect and feelings can be influenced by conscious manipulation of the behavior expressed in the face and body. If I "whistle a happy tune" when I feel afraid, I "fool myself as well."[4] If I hold my head up and smile as I walk down the street, I will feel less depressed than if I slouch, frown, and stare at the sidewalk.

Cognition: Cognition is defined as an idea, thought, or memory without an emotion or feeling attached to it. Cognition can refer to a thought in the form of a mental statement such as "two plus two equals four." It is clear to all how this statement could be made out loud or thought silently without any feeling attached to it. But cognition could also refer to the statement, "There is a dangerous stranger hiding in our house." Most will understand how it would be difficult to think this without feelings of fear or anger. For the purposes of this book, however, we will consider that the thought is neutral and the feeling is attached to it. We will say that the cognition (thought) is associated with the affect (emotion). Some often repeated statements, self-critical statements in particular, can become associated with a strong affective response. The association is a connection that works two ways. When I tell myself, "I am really stupid," I evoke the affect of shame. And when some other event triggers shame, the thought that springs to mind is, "I am really stupid."

Cognition can also be understood as a remembered or imagined picture, movie, or sound. If I think there is a dangerous stranger hiding in my house, I begin a visual scan of my house to imagine where this stranger might be lurking. Such visual imagery powerfully evokes an emotional response, but we will consider the imagery to be a form of cognition separate from the affect that is evoked. Differentiating cognition and affect will prove useful in changing the ways that affect influences thinking and behavior.

Evolution: A third word, evolution, is familiar to most people in its primary meaning, that of biological evolution. In Chapter 3, we will be talking about the biological evolution of the primary emotions and their survival value for individuals. The part of the brain that is the seat of the primary emotions is the brain stem, which is responsible for controlling physical movement, reactions, and reflexes, of which the emotions are an integral part. The basic capacities for movement, reactions, and emotions that have evolved in the brain stem are hardwired in all animals and have not changed for many thousands of years.

I will also be referring to a less familiar type of evolution, cultural evolution. In addition to the brain stem, where our basic reactions and primary emotions are hardwired, humans have evolved a large neocortex, the part of the brain capable of analysis, synthesis, problem solving, and complex memory. The neocortex allows us to adapt to a wide variety of

Introduction

environmental situations by learning and memorizing the behaviors that work best in the situations we face most often. The infant is born with the basic capacities installed in the brain stem but also with the capacity to learn behaviors that work best for the environment he finds himself born into. Language, social customs, and many important survival facts will be learned by each child in the first few years of life, and this body of learning will be shaped by the accumulated experience of preceding generations. For example, the Inuit baby raised in an icy climate by a family that depends on hunting and fishing for survival will learn to recognize and name many different kinds of snow because the differences are important to his family's survival. The same baby raised in a tropical climate would learn nothing at all about snow.

The tremendous adaptive capacity of the neocortex allows for new learning to be passed down from one generation to the next and for the total mass of adaptive information to change and grow—to evolve—as new solutions are found for the problems of survival and the challenges of living together in societies. These social challenges have special significance for our topic of criticism, as we will discuss in the next chapter.

Despite the powerful learning capacity of the neocortex, however, the primary emotional responses remain hardwired in the brainstem. Affect influences our thinking and thinking can influence affect in a complex interaction between the brain stem and the neocortex, much of which is learned. With experience, we can learn to use memory and analysis to inhibit or stimulate emotional responses, but not to eliminate them. Thus, we can learn to manage our emotions, but we cannot manage our lives without them.

My hope is that this book will help you understand the interplay of shame and anger that is almost universal in critical interaction, and that this understanding, along with some of the techniques presented, will help you experience and respond to criticism more comfortably and effectively. As a result of that, I hope you will also be able to become a more skillful and sensitive parent, teacher, supervisor, partner, friend, and critic.

Chapter Two

Our Problems with Criticism

Criticism or perceived criticism appears almost daily throughout our lives in a variety of interactions and situations. Do any of the following scenarios sound familiar to you?

Eight year old Jake completes a homework assignment and shows it confidently to his mother. She finds a small mistake and starts to show him how to correct it. But when she points it out, he tears up the paper in frustration and is inconsolable for the next hour.

Cindy, trying on several prom dresses in a boutique, becomes increasingly irritable when her mother comments on which ones are more flattering.

Geoff offers constructive criticism to a supervisee, but meets with nothing but defensive excuses and arguments.

Our Problems with Criticism

George is confronted by his wife because she is worried about his drinking and driving, especially when he is with the children. He shouts obscenities at her and stalks out, slamming the door hard enough to crack the frame.

Valerie listens to her friend, Sue, complain about Valerie's habitual tardiness and concludes that Sue is being unreasonable and controlling.

Giving and accepting criticism gracefully can be tricky business. Many a friendship or family relationship has foundered on the shoals of major, minor, or even anticipated criticism. Performance evaluations at school or work are minefields of misunderstood criticism. Intimate relationships, once contaminated with real or anticipated criticism, can be poisoned with hurt or anger. Adolescents subjected to teasing in the brutal social competition of middle school years, may form distorted self-images based on the careless criticism of their peers. Patterns of criticism and reaction to criticism between young adults and their parents or in-laws can establish negative expectations that freeze the relationships in habits of mutual avoidance or conflict that can last for years.

When we are giving criticism, we may think we are giving friendly, helpful, or objective feedback to someone and be surprised when he responds negatively. We may think we have the right to influence someone's behavior by telling her how she is wrong, and we are likely to be irritated if our opinion is rejected. When we are angry or frustrated, we may express our criticism as a rude complaint without any helpful intention or real expectation of change, or we may angrily demand change in response to our criticism.

When we are on the receiving end of such criticism, however, we frequently react as though it is a painful attack, even if the critic is not rude, angry, or demanding.

Criticism can be useful

When we look at it objectively, the criticism we receive can be understood as observations and opinions about us and our behavior from someone else's point of view, and there are many times when we could benefit from listening to another point of view. There are times when we ask for it and even times when we pay for it. We hire golf professionals to criticize our swing, consultants to analyze our business plans, and trainers to improve the productivity of our work teams. How are they to do their jobs without some form of critical feedback? In cases like these we hope that someone with more experience and skill can look at our performance and give us some helpful tips based on their objective and informed point of view. When we ask for criticism, we may be able to accept it graciously. In such cases, of course, we get to choose the critic and the scope of the criticism. We even feel confident that we are free to accept or reject it.

But we also know we are going to receive criticism when we don't ask for it, so perhaps our problem is with unsolicited criticism. In each of the five examples given earlier in the chapter the comments that were perceived as criticism were initiated by the critic, and that is the way it happens most of the time. We do not wait for our children to ask for criticism on their manners. We don't expect teachers to be silent until students ask for their input. We generally want honest feedback from those we love and trust the most. It is understood to be part of the responsibility of teachers, parents, supervisors, coaches, spouses, and good friends to provide what we call constructive criticism as a normal function of their relationship with us and ours with them. Nonetheless, unsolicited criticism frequently hurts, no matter who gives it.

What makes our experience of criticism so painful?

Why does it hurt so much when we receive criticism, and how can we control these hurt feelings to render them less painful and aversive? The primary focus of this book will be on the experience of receiving criticism and the problematic emotional reactions we often have when receiving it. What is it about criticism that causes us to perceive it as an attack?

Our Problems with Criticism

The difficulty we face in learning to handle criticism stems from the fact that, early in life, criticism becomes associated with two of our most powerful and basic emotions—shame and anger.

We learn at an early age to react to criticism with these powerful emotions, and most of us do not fully learn an alternative response as we grow older. The reasons for this will be detailed in the next three chapters. Shame and anger almost always come into play when we are receiving criticism, though for some, the expectation of punishment can be so intense that fear is also evoked. Sometimes the shame is experienced as mild embarrassment or chagrin, but sometimes it can be experienced as horrifying guilt. Sometimes the anger is a brief irritation, but sometimes it can be a rage that blinds us to the potential truth in the criticism we are hearing.

When certain kinds of events become associated with specific emotions, our perception of similar events is influenced by that emotional response. We sometimes speak of viewing events through an emotional lens. If we are feeling angry or threatened when we bump into someone in a crowd, we are more likely to jump to the conclusion that their carelessness or bad intention was to blame. If we are feeling confused or self-conscious, we are more likely to assume that it was our fault. As such, our perception of criticism is influenced by the emotional response we have to criticism we receive, with the end result being that we can perceive it as more threatening or punishing than the critic intends.

When Ellen was not given the part she wanted in the class play, she told her mother that the drama teacher didn't like her. In her disappointment, she attributed a punishing intent to the teacher's decision to give the part to someone else. Although no criticism was actually given in this case, shame and anger were experienced because Ellen assumed she had been criticized.

Most of us don't like to receive criticism, particularly unsolicited criticism, so it seems obvious that we would react to

13

criticism with an unpleasant emotional response. But occasionally we meet someone who manages to listen to criticism seriously, without reacting with shame or anger, even when the criticism is harsh. Such a person has somehow learned to view criticism as potentially useful information from a different perspective than his own, and to hear it without the strong visceral and negative reaction many of us experience.

Those of us who haven't mastered such an enlightened response are likely to continue to feel attacked, ashamed, guilty, disrespected, and/or angry. Usually we react with these feelings instantly before we have had a chance to evaluate the clarity or meaning of the critic's point of view, much less its potential value to us.

If we want to learn how to use the criticism we receive to our own best advantage without suffering excessive emotional swings of shame and anger, we can benefit from the growing body of concepts known as "emotional intelligence," which offer us valuable tools for dealing with our own powerful emotional responses.

And if we aspire to become a sensitive and effective critic, teacher, supervisor, parent, spouse or friend, we can benefit from understanding the emotional dynamics of shame and anger that tend to dominate any critical interaction.

The Role of Personal Values in Criticism

A lot of the criticism we give and receive has its roots in differences in personal values, standards, or preferences. If I prefer hip hop and my roommate prefers classical music, he may perceive my distaste for classical music as criticism. If I expect him to share my preference and disparage his tastes, that perception is confirmed. We are entitled to our own values and standards, likes and dislikes, as long as we do not seek to force others to agree. It is inevitable that we will want others to share our preferences, however, and this can lead to judging and criticizing others' values.

Each of us is ultimately the most important judge of our own values, standards, and behavior. If I assume that my critic is a more important judge, then I must accept the criticism without question. But if I am my own judge, and I want to learn from the observations and opinions of others, I can consider the evidence and make the best decision possible about the criticism I receive. Such an attitude toward criticism is based in certain principles of assertiveness that emphasize our individual right to and responsibility for our own values. We will address these principles more thoroughly in Chapters 9 and 10. If I disagree with someone else's values or behavior, I can explain my own values, hoping to influence him, or at least to get him to accept my right to choose. I can ask someone to do something because of my preferences, my needs, or my values. But whether they agree to do so or not is their right, their decision, and their responsibility.

Jim prefers a tidy house. Jill is not so particular, preferring to spend her energy painting and sketching. If Jim resents the fact that Jill doesn't do the dishes and calls her a lazy slob, he is assuming that she shares his values and that she is not taking responsibility for her behavior. It may be, however, that Jill really doesn't care at all about a tidy house and places no value on washing the dishes. If Jim recognizes this, he can still ask her for help, saying, "I realize you don't care about the dishes, but I do, and I would appreciate your help." Jill can agree to help without changing or violating her values about tidiness, but if she is in the middle of a painting, she could also say, "This painting is more important to me right now. I'll help later." Jim, acting assertively, can try to persuade her or try to reach a compromise, but if he crosses the line into intimidation or manipulation by disparaging Jill's values or blasting her with punitive criticism, he risks winning a battle but losing a piece of the relationship. If Jill agrees, only to avoid a punishing scene, she will resent it later and cooperation will deteriorate.

Criticism is usually offered after the fact, after the homework has been forgotten or the trash man has come and gone without the waste basket being emptied. When we hear criticism, it is safe to assume that we are failing to meet

Chapter Two

someone's expectations (those of the critic) or that we have transgressed or ignored their values. Their criticism tells us they are concerned enough about this to say something. We usually pay attention to this because we learn early in life to pay attention to our parent's expectations as well as those of other important people in our environment. We have an emotional reaction that alerts us and raises our attention level when we are criticized. It is the complex nature of this emotional reaction that is the focus of this book.

The Origins and Importance of Social Standards

Understanding the standards and expectations of others is necessary to achieve some degree of social order, which is an appropriate survival concern for all human societies. If everyone acted spontaneously or without reference to any common set of standards or expectations, social life would be chaos. Everyone would be on guard for the worst behavior in others, and this extreme defensiveness would make us all much more dangerous.

Jared Diamond makes the point in his book, Guns, Germs, and Steel,[5] that organized societies developed because of their survival value. He describes the evolution of chiefdoms, states, and nations, attributing the trend toward greater social organization to the survival value of such organizations. If two members of unrelated hunter-gatherer tribes encounter one another in the wilderness of Borneo, they may well try to kill one another in preemptive self-defense. When individuals are raised in a large tribe with the understanding that you do not kill members of your own tribe, the larger tribe has an advantage over a smaller one. This is a matter of cultural evolution rather than biological evolution. It is a learned pattern of behavior that is deeply instilled into the members of the culture because it has significance for the survival of the tribe or society. Most members of a tribe raised with this social standard will learn to associate a sense of horror with the killing of members of their own group and learn it so thoroughly that the powerful emotional reaction is difficult to distinguish from an instinct hardwired in the brain stem. There are always some individuals who do not learn and are therefore violent and unsocialized, but it is in the interest of the tribe to control them. They are criticized, censured, and excluded if they continue behavior that is dangerous to the tribe. Although as individuals we may be hardwired for violent self-defense, we are responsive to intensive social training and pressure from birth to accept the standards and values of the society in which we are raised. As a result, we become sensitive, sometimes oversensitive, to the expectations of others in general.

In stable and functional societies, there is a core set of basic values and standards that allow us to live together successfully. But there are also many subtle differences in preferences or expectations that are possible between individuals within a single functional and stable society. When all differences are suppressed those same communities risk becoming rigid and are unable to adapt to changing times and needs. Historically, societies that are rigidly intolerant of differences lose their creativity and adaptability and eventually fail. Therefore, while it is important to understand and follow the general standards and expectations of one's social environment, it is neither possible nor desirable to meet all of the expectations of others in an open and healthy social order. In such a society, individuals are expected to understand the basic expectations of living together while taking responsibility for many of their own personal preferences and personal values.

Value Conflicts

We have a lot of personal preferences and values that have little to do with survival in the circumstances most of us inhabit in modern times. And we often have strong feelings about these preferences and values, even when they can be shown to be superficial or even irrational. It is as if our primitive genetic predisposition to fear of strangers, suspicion of the different, "the other," is always in conflict with our learned ability to override this fear for the sake of the survival advantage of social order. Yet it is easy to demonstrate that these personal preferences and values are culturally transmitted. We are not born with them but learn them in the bosom of our families or in the classroom or in all the other ways we absorb the values of our cultures.

We can not know for sure how this mass of culturally transmitted preferences and values came to be and how they became so emotionally charged for us. But we can speculate, taking our lead from the kind of argument Diamond makes in <u>Guns, Germs, and Steel</u>, and that other cultural anthropologists have confirmed in their research.

When humans lived in small, nomadic hunter-gatherer tribes or clans of herdsmen, their survival depended on being able to quickly differentiate friend from foe, safety from threat. When humans learned to cultivate crops and domesticate animals, they settled in larger and larger communities, eventually gathering together in cities and states that were centers of wealth and trade. At some point, you no longer knew everyone in your community and had to assume they were safe if they dressed the same as you, spoke the same as you, or looked the same as you. Otherwise, they might be dangerous aliens. At this stage of cultural evolution, humans were not that far from the primitive stage of preemptive self-defense, but they had learned that we can only live together successfully in larger communities if we do not kill our neighbors. But how do I know that this odd looking fellow I haven't seen before is my neighbor? How do I know he knows the rules and won't kill me? This question awakens primitive survival emotions and focuses them on increasingly subtle judgments about who is my friend and who is my foe. The criteria for these subtle judgments are taught to children and passed on in the culture of the community, city, or state to permit social cooperation while maintaining the security perimeter of the now very large and diverse group.

This ability to learn to make and apply a great many subtle judgments through the power of the analytical neocortex is thus linked to the powerful primitive emotional equipment centered in the brain stem that enabled us to survive before there were cities and states. As cities grew larger and societies more diverse, the ability to make these subtle judgments seems to have evolved (culturally) to a new level of magnitude. Not only do we discern friend from foe, but also master from servant, ally from competitor, and a whole continuum of shades of similarity or difference that are tinged with a sense of threat or safety. We make quick judgments about whose company we prefer, whose dress, whose speech, whose hair or skin color, whose customs or manners, whose cuisine, etc. And all of the judgments we make about these differences are shaded with those survival emotions that make the "other" feel threatening.

On the one hand, we are taught, more by imitating the choices we see acted out in our culture than by active teaching, the preferences and values we grow up with. On the other hand, we are also taught to want to fit in to our own society, to cooperate, and to expect others to do the same. As a result of the latter, we often expect others to share more of our preferences and values than is really required for a healthy social order. We tend to think that our own way is the "right" way and that the other way is not just "different" but "wrong." This tendency or expectation is connected, by a long chain of biological and cultural evolution, to a basic sense of safety or threat that makes our rightness or our differentness feel crucial.

Anyone who tries to accept all of the different values and expectations of everyone they know out of a need for social conformity will be up against an impossible situation. Trying to be all things to all people will make you crazy. Each of us must have a method for choosing which values to respect, what criticism to accept, what values and criticism to reject, and what criticism to simply ignore. The latter is particularly important when we find ourselves subjected to emotional bullying that is clearly calculated to intimidate, or to criticism that is so unrealistic or unclear that it is impossible to interpret and evaluate. The ability to suspend the shame response in such circumstances is essential for the maintenance of self-esteem.

Jeanne was a new associate at an advertising agency and was assigned to some existing accounts with especially demanding customers. One of the customers routinely responded to her presentations by dismissing her work as worthless, but Jeanne could never get this customer to give her a clear idea of what approach he was looking for. The customer's tirades were consistently nasty and lacking in specifics. She began to feel that she was missing something important or that her skills were seriously lacking. Finally, one of the more experienced hands at the agency told her that this customer treated everyone this way, especially new female associates. Eventually, the customer would accept the proposal but was never complimentary. Assignment to this account was an ordeal to which new associates were often subjected in order to test their ability to produce under pressure. This knowledge enabled Jeanne to continue working with this customer without sustaining further doubts about her own ability.

Since it is impossible to live up to everyone's expectations, it is important to determine whether we understand and agree with a critic's expectations before we can decide what to make of the criticism. It can be a respectful and powerful response to criticism to say, "I've thought about what you said, and I understand what you think I should have done in that situation, but I just don't agree. We have different values on this matter." Of course it is also powerful to be able to say, sincerely, "I agree with your criticism and I am going to try harder in the future to meet that expectation because I believe in it, too."

Shame and Disrespect

Sometimes criticism is assumed or perceived, not because of overtly hostile or critical words or actions, but because of a lack of overt recognition or show of respect. A great deal of shame and anger is experienced in response to what has become known as disrespect or "dissing." Since hip hop culture popularized the term in recent years, the word has become familiar in the wider American culture as a way of describing a subtle and common insult, the failure to recognize and show respect for another individual.

The need for recognition is universal. When someone we know passes us without greeting or someone looks through us as if we aren't there, we often feel belittled, even if the slight is unintended. An introverted person who has difficulty making eye contact can be perceived to be arrogant, particularly if she is

Our Problems with Criticism

in a position of authority. An anxious person who needs to control his environment and the people in it in order to feel safe can be perceived as dismissive of others' preferences or opinions. All but the most sensitive among us are likely to be guilty of this kind of unintentional disrespect occasionally, but those who find themselves overlooked, ignored, subordinated, or dismissed, often feel the sting of shame and anger as if they had been overtly criticized or attacked. Because this inferred criticism is unspoken, it is difficult to analyze or confront, but can still be an insidious source of pain. Members of minority groups who experience themselves as invisible to the majority public have expressed this pain. Individuals who, for one reason or another, grow up anxious to please others find themselves excruciatingly sensitive to signs of disrespect and easily read into it evidence of criticism. Overt or covert, intended or not, constructive or otherwise, criticism evokes a painful reaction.

Whether or not we think we can benefit from criticism, we are all going to get plenty of it and we might as well learn how to handle it effectively. Shame and anger will inevitably be involved, and these powerful emotional responses so confuse and overwhelm our experience of criticism that we will have difficulty responding objectively and effectively.

Before we look at shame and anger separately and in their connection to one another, we need to discuss the evolutionary significance of the set of affects that are hardwired in the brain stem and understand why they have such immediate power to influence our behavior and our thinking.

Chapter Three
Powerful Primary Emotions

We are highly evolved animals, but we are animals nonetheless. Our brains, nervous systems, hormonal systems, and musculature have evolved into a complex system that provides us with automatic, rapid responses to situations that are important for our physical survival. We are aware of this complex system of nervous and physical responses as emotions or feelings. We notice the sensations associated with emotional states and can learn to recognize and name them. We may realize that they guide our decisions and behavior constantly, often without our conscious awareness. But we are more likely to place feelings and actions in different categories as if feelings are ephemeral and therefore less significant than actions. The truth is that strong emotions compel us to act. Feelings and actions are almost inseparable. Understanding the survival value of this connection highlights the power and immediacy of our emotional reactions. This makes it clear how important it is to understand our emotions. As we briefly discussed in Chapter 1,

Powerful Primary Emotions

the part of our brain that generates these emotional responses (the brain stem) is older, in terms of evolution, than the part that allows us to analyze complex situations and plan detailed solutions (the neocortex). Our actions are more immediately and powerfully influenced by the more primitive part of our brain.

These primary emotional responses have been studied by affect theorists. Each affect is recognizable as a distinct facial expression in very young infants, and each has significant survival value for the individual. Some of these hardwired affects are listed below. The two words describing each affect represent two ends of a continuum of a distinct affect or emotion.

Interest – Excitement

Enjoyment – Joy

Surprise – Startle

Distress – Anguish

Fear – Terror

Anger – Rage

Shame – Humiliation[6]

The emotions or affects of "interest," "enjoyment," and "distress," have survival value for us as social animals who must communicate with those closest to us in order to have our needs met. Interest and excitement have survival value in helping us focus our attention. Enjoyment and joy have survival value in communicating recognition of friends, pleasure, and in discharging more stressful emotional states. Distress communicates our need for comfort. The facial expression of "surprise" has functional value by increasing our alertness and perceptivity when startled. The eyebrows are raised, allowing in more light, and the eyes blink clearing the vision.

Chapter Three

"Fear" and "anger" are perhaps the most familiar of our basic emotions. Although we may not fully understand the causes and the power of these emotions, we recognize them easily in ourselves and others. Because the part of the brain responsible for these responses is an old part, similar to the structure of the brain stems of other animals, the physical responses and the signals are similar. We have no difficulty recognizing and distinguishing the behavior of an angry dog from that of a fearful dog because our emotional brain stems evolved from the same limb of the evolutionary tree, so the body language of an angry or fearful dog is familiar to us at a very basic level.

The survival significance of fear and anger are also easy to understand. They each generate intense responses that prepare us to deal with the physical demands of an emergency, as well as sending unmistakable signals to others nearby regarding our aroused emotional and physical state. Fear compels us first to freeze, to try to become invisible, and then to run like crazy. We freeze, instinctively, to camouflage us from the perceived predator. Meanwhile, the heart rate increases, and blood flow is directed to the large muscles necessary for running. The tension between the aroused nervous system and muscles while we are frozen "like a deer in the headlights" causes us to tremble. And the fact that blood flow has been directed to the large running and fighting muscles and away from the digestive tract, causes us to feel cold or uncomfortable in the pit of our stomach. The eyes are wide open to let in more light, so that we can be even more alert to the approach of danger.

Anger is similarly familiar in its effect on us. The blood flow is redirected as with fear, but with even more emphasis on the arms, hands, and jaw for use in fighting rather than running. The brow is lowered to protect the eyes and the eyes are focused glaringly on the enemy. Adrenalin pours into our blood stream to empower extreme action in the service of survival.

Understanding the primitive power of our emotional brains can give us an advantage in tuning and attenuating our emotional and compulsive responses to certain situations.

Powerful Primary Emotions

Daniel Goleman's books on emotional intelligence help us to understand that these powerful emotions are designed for "quick and dirty" response.[7] In a survival situation, we cannot wait for a detailed analysis of a complex situation. We must act quickly and energetically in order to survive or prevail. The basic emotions are the business of the brain stem, the most rudimentary part of the brain, and the part most immediately involved in controlling the body.

The bad news is that these quick and dirty emotional responses can often misfire and do a lot of damage in the delicately balanced social networks that make up civilized life.

> "It was a tragedy of errors. Fourteen-year-old Matilda Crabtree was just playing a practical joke on her father. She jumped out of a closet and yelled 'Boo!' as her parents came home at one in the morning from visiting friends. But Bobby Crabtree and his wife thought Matilda was staying with friends that night. Hearing noises as he entered the house, Crabtree reached for his .357 caliber pistol and went into Matilda's bedroom to investigate. When his daughter jumped from the closet, Crabtree shot her in the neck. Matilda Crabtree died twelve hours later. Fear primed Crabtree to shoot before he could fully register what he was shooting at, before he could recognize his daughter's voice. Automatic reactions of this sort have become etched in our nervous system, evolutionary biologists presume, because for a long and crucial period in human prehistory they made the difference between survival and death."[8]

Although the example noted above is tragic, the fact is that we still sometimes need all the power of an immediate passionate emotional response in order to cope with extreme situations. As an enlisted man in the Coast Guard, my son sometimes had the duty to dive off of a rescue cutter in 20 foot seas and swim to the victims of a foundering fishing boat with a life line. This is an extreme survival situation indeed. A disciplined team of trained rescue professionals must face the powerful and dangerous forces of nature. The mission of rescue is supported and accomplished by an experienced group in which the individual can have some confidence. But the civilized institution of the Coast Guard did not exist when our brains and emotional reactions were evolving. The task of swimming in storm seas still requires the physical response appropriate to a life and death emergency, even if you are tethered to the team by a life line. Powerful primary emotions are designed for just such emergencies. Adrenaline pumped into the bloodstream in response to fear fires the large muscles for quick and violent action. Consciousness is focused on a simple goal. Every resource in the body and mind is focused on the immediate need. In such circumstances, I want my son, or any rescuer, to instantly have all of the adrenaline and sense of emergency that his brain and body can produce.

Though our complex brains have these powerful emotions hardwired into the brain stem, there is more to the brain than just the stem. We also have higher brain functions housed in the neocortex, the top layers of the brain that evolved later to enable thinking, language, and planning, and that allow us to learn complex new responses to complex new situations.

The good news is that it is possible to learn skills that allow us to balance passion with judgment, even if most of us will not be able to eliminate the passionate response to certain urgent stimuli. Recent studies of Buddhist monks with many years of disciplined practice at meditation have shown them to have a remarkable ability to override a flinch reaction to a loud sudden noise that neurologists previously considered to be humanly impossible.[9] Though this degree of self-control is not necessary to learn how to respond thoughtfully to criticism, it does indicate the amazing adaptability of the brain.

An important part of the learning necessary to take advantage of these higher functions lies in understanding our own emotions. Most of us understand fear and anger reasonably well, even if we don't always succeed in controlling them. But we have another emotion, equally important, that is not so well understood. This is the affect or emotion we call shame.

Chapter Four
What is Shame?

Shame is included among the fundamental emotions described by affect theorists and resembles fear and anger in its intensity. It is a universal human experience, and we all know something about what shame feels like. But what is the survival value of shame? Why are we hardwired with this uncomfortable emotional response?

Pain motivates us to favor an injured limb, anger motivates us to attack, and fear motivates us to freeze first and prepare to run. Similarly, shame motivates us and our fellow mammals to signal surrender in order to survive when the odds against us are too great. Under the influence of the affect of shame, we hide from the gaze of the attacker, and, by averting our own gaze, avoid challenging and antagonizing that attacker. The bowed head is the classic demonstration of inferiority seen in many animals when they are overwhelmed in a fight or threatened with overwhelming force.

Chapter Four

Other animals understand the body language of shame and aggression, even when it is displayed by another species. At the National Zoo in Washington, DC, a few blocks from where I live, instructions for visitors to the great ape house inform us that we should approach the cages backward, glancing at the apes over our shoulders, rather than approaching them frontally and staring at them, because the apes interpret frontal staring as aggression. If you stare directly at the younger apes, they will begin to wave their arms, shriek and leap about in demonstrations of threatening and aggressive behavior. The 800 pound papa gorilla, confident in his own power, sits politely with his back to the glass wall so that he will not intimidate the puny human visitors.

The facial expression of shame—eyes down or averted, head bowed—can be seen whenever you frown and stare at an infant or speak harshly to a toddler. The averted gaze inspires the phrase "loss of face," characteristic of humiliation. It is seen in the carvings on ancient Egyptian temples, powerfully portraying the superiority of pharaoh and the submission of his enemies. It is the classic posture of bowing or other gestures of obeisance demonstrating respect for a ruler or loyalty to a deity.

Shame, then, can be understood as the affect of surrender, the human emotional analog to the surrender instinct commonly seen in other animals. For many animal species, the ability to clearly signal "you have won and I have lost" is crucial to survival. It is the reason that animals seldom fight to the death except when hunting for food. And it is the mechanism that allows the majority of non-dominant animals to survive the competition within their species. The dog that lowers its head, tucks its tail between its legs, and slinks away survives a battle over turf.

The young human being in a primitive tribal group shows deference or respect for the stronger members of the tribe by displaying the facial expression or body posture of obeisance or surrender in a confrontation. If he does not, he risks being cast out or killed because order and hierarchy in primitive social groups is vitally important.

What is Shame?

Shame, as the affect of surrender or deference, plays a central function in group, tribe, or family dynamics. For humans, and other primates that live in communities or extended family groups, the group itself is a survival advantage. Social hierarchy fosters effective cooperation and establishes a leadership structure that is an essential for the group to survive and thrive. In dangerous circumstances where effective group functioning is a matter of life or death for the whole tribe, it is imperative that we understand instinctively the postures of shame and dominance. So we come into the world equipped with the capacity for shame whether our environmental circumstances are dangerous or safe. We respond instinctively with feelings, facial expressions, and postures of shame when we are threatened.

Because cooperation is vital for the survival of the group, children are trained from infancy to respect its social hierarchy, values, and customs. The long period of dependency of young humans and other higher primates provides time for the young to learn the complex social order and values necessary to function as members of the group. The affect of shame is one of the emotional mechanisms that reinforces that respect for order and group values, and thereby ensures that members behave within certain limits consistent with the welfare of the group.

This learning accumulates through years of experiences interacting with mature members of the primal group (parents, for example) who may scold or punish behavior that transgresses group values. It continues through the formation of the other social hierarchies in our lives—the playground, the teen clique, the office structure. Through this process, a collection of memories, habits, and values is formed that we sometimes call our conscience. Some of these memories include a touch of the shame associated with past experiences of scolding. This serves as a hint of warning when we are contemplating behavior unacceptable to the group. Other memories include positive examples of approved behavior that serve as models for acceptable action. This set of memories, this conscience, is so thoroughly internalized by constant practice that we come to think of it as a part of our personality or character, our own private set of values.

So the evolution moves from that of the physical—the brain and nervous system equipped with primal emotions—to the social—the transmission of social conventions we need for our group functioning to succeed. We begin as very young children to learn who we are and how we feel about ourselves as we negotiate life with our basic emotional tools. Our identity, the self with whom we are so familiar, develops as a collection of habits of response that we work out by trial and error, by observation and imitation in interaction with our social environment, and with the basic emotional equipment with which we are born.

Shame is intensified by exposure

Just as the affect of shame compels us to surrender and retreat, it also compels us to hide. We want to become invisible, at least for awhile. Being exposed or being viewed as a loser intensifies the affect of shame. In a primitive animal context, visibility as a loser creates greater dangers. In a human social context, there are social dangers.

The etymological root of the word, shame, means "to cover" and our worst fear when we hide our shame is that we will be "dis-covered." [10]

This aspect of the physical expression of shame was described by Charles Darwin in 1872.

> "Under a keen sense of shame, there is a strong desire for concealment. We turn away the whole body, more especially the face, which we endeavor in some manner to hide. An ashamed person can hardly endure to meet the gaze of those present, so that he almost invariably casts down his eyes or looks askant." [11]

The painting on the cover of this book includes the portrait of a boy in the far left corner demonstrating the classic posture and facial expression of shame.

What is Shame?

Public shaming is a well known part of punishment in social environments. School children have been punished by being seated in the front of the class wearing a "dunce cap." In colonial times, in Europe and America, miscreants were pilloried in the town square, exposed to the view and censure of the public. Enemies of the Roman Empire were mocked with derisive labels when they were hung naked and helpless on a cross to die slowly of asphyxiation. The exposure not only intensified the shame of the one being executed, but also sent a public message to all of his associates: you who associate yourselves with this one stand at risk of similar humiliation and death.

Frank, like all of us, had thought and done things for which he believed he could be criticized. He had, for example, procrastinated projects as a student and later as a worker, sometimes telling "white lies" to excuse his tardiness. He had hurt the feelings of friends and family members by being insensitive at times. He had imagined getting revenge for slights or hurts done to him, and his imagination provided him with gruesome means for revenge. He had even participated in tormenting less popular kids in school when that was part of the expectation to gain group acceptance. Without understanding that shame was motivating him, Frank began to pretend that he was the kind of person who would never think or do these things. He presented to the world the image of a man who was never greedy, never dishonest, never unworthy. And secretly, he came to believe that he could not, would not, and should not be accepted and respected by his fellow man if he was in any way greedy, dishonest, or unworthy. But in his heart of hearts, he knew he was lying, knew that he was hiding these things, that he was covering up. And he was afraid of being discovered. He lived behind the mask of a false self, a noble presentation that he showed to the world because he believed the world would not accept or respect him as he was, with all his common faults. Because he was secretly afraid of being discovered and rejected, he could not put down his mask. It was as if he was the victim of a blackmailer who knew something awful about him and threatened to reveal it. But the blackmailer was his own conscience, and the payment his conscience demanded was that he live with ongoing shame, fear, and anger. Frank didn't understand the trap he was in. The powerful basic emotions that kept him imprisoned were able to persist because he could not think about or talk about his shame.

Why don't we talk about shame?

Confusion about morality

There is a lot of confusion about shame that hinders us in dealing with this powerful emotion.

Many people confuse the emotion of shame with the moral state of being guilty. Our language does not have a clear and concise way of differentiating between "I feel ashamed" and "I am guilty." The moral state of guilt might be explained this way: "I know that I have done something that I believe was wrong. I have failed to behave according to my own beliefs about what is right." The bad feeling that often colors this "knowledge" is shame; shame about personal failure to do the right thing. It is not the same as the feeling of shame about being caught and exposed, though both feelings are variations of shame. When a confessed felon is required to acknowledge his crime in open court in front of the victim or relatives of the victim, part of what is going on is a careful scrutiny of the voice tone, choice of words, body language, and facial expressions of the felon to determine whether there is genuine remorse, a recognition of the failure to do the right thing, and the appropriate affect of surrender to society as opposed to shame over the failure to escape discovery, public censure, and punishment.

To analyze the emotion of shame may seem to threaten the foundations of our morality. Some may fear that learning to control shame may lead to an erosion of conscience creating a population of psychopaths, people with no consciences whatsoever. I am inclined to believe the opposite is true. The conscience is truly damaged when there is no sense of basic trust or expectation of reconciliation or redemption. If a person believes the whole world is his enemy, he will not feel bound by conscience or moral obligation. He will constantly feel like an escaped prisoner behind enemy lines. This is the amoral position of the psychopath. The hope of belonging, the possibility of reconciliation to a cherished individual or group can be a powerful motivator to treat others well. The balance of shame and reconciliation, sin and redemption, justice and mercy, are the sticks and carrots that keep us working together.

We may feel ashamed to talk about shame.

As Kaufman points out, we don't much like to talk about this particular emotion, perhaps because talking about shame tends to evoke some of the sting of this powerful and painful feeling.[12] Many of our basic affective states seem to have an infectious or contagious quality to them. There is a universal tendency to suppress expression of powerful affect in public—perhaps because its expression can be contagious. For example, when we see terror on the face of someone in proximity to us, it is a natural response to feel anxiety in ourselves. The escalation of panic in a crowd can be catastrophic, as can the escalation of rage into mob violence.

Shame and distress are similarly contagious, especially within the primary groups with which we identify: our families. When we see the posture and facial expression of shame on the face of our parent or our child, we often identify and feel the shame ourselves. It is our own internal distress in response to the crying child that motivates us to want to comfort him. And most of us cannot watch a scene of abject humiliation without some twinge of empathic embarrassment or defensive anger. Like the victim, we want to avert our eyes and turn away.

As we have discussed, shame motivates us first to hide, to avoid eye contact, and to keep quiet, though the anger response that follows may motivate us to protest. It may be that this contagious and uncomfortable response to shame, even as a subject for discussion, is part of the reason we do not talk about it.

Chapter Four

As a result, we don't understand it well.

According to Kaufman, there is a "lack of an adequate language" to talk about and understand shame. Without sufficiently detailed concepts, or words with a clear, comfortable, and common reference, talking about shame causes us to make pictures in our own mind or replay tapes of past experience involving shame.[13]   Such images evoke the feelings of shame associated with the experience, and make us uncomfortable. So we are more likely than not to avoid them. As long as we continue to avoid these feelings, however, we will fail to understand them and fail to learn to deal with them effectively. Perhaps the reader has noticed memories associated with shame cropping up in response to the examples or the discussion in this chapter. The ability to recognize this feeling, label it, and understand its power, is a step in the direction of self-awareness, an essential element in emotional intelligence.

Why should we talk about shame?

The basic emotion of shame is at the root of a tremendous amount of human suffering and miscommunication. We human beings live our entire lives in relationships—relationships with ourselves and our families and larger communities. Shame has a function in shaping our awareness of all of these relationships. It also has terrible potential to damage them, even the very private relationship with ourselves.

John Bradshaw, in the introduction to his popular book, Healing the Shame that Binds You, refers to shame as "the core demon in my life and one of the major destructive forces in all human life."[14] Kaufman notes that, "Shame is the affect which is the source of many complex and disturbing inner states."[15]

Early in life, the painful emotion of shame makes us hide our mistakes and blame others rather than taking responsibility for learning from them. Shameful hiding or angry blaming can become a habitual response to situations that evoke shame. Angry blaming (a response closely related to shame that we will explore in detail later) can lead to the kind of harsh criticism that makes others want to hide their mistakes or pass the blame further down the line.

When people spend time blaming and embarrassing their opponents in public debate, there is less time and motivation for productive compromise. When political leaders seek to increase their power by blaming their opponents for realities their opponents cannot control, they are manipulating the powerful basic emotions of shame, fear, and anger in the public forum. The result is that the discussion of complex problems is oversimplified and distorted. Public discourse degenerates under the pressure of shame into a persistent battle of shifting the blame for problems rather than a productive exploration of potential solutions.

On the other hand, we often learn to blame ourselves in a way that undermines self-esteem and creates a hypersensitivity to criticism and a fear of being judged or even observed. When this learned fear is intense enough and habitual enough it can inhibit or complicate healthy expression of normal behaviors, including even our most basic drives such as eating and healthy sexuality.

Some individuals with eating disorders have learned to associate intense shame over weight and body image with the act of eating. An association of this kind is a learned stimulus-response pattern in that the experience of one part of the association will remind the individual of the other part. When the intense feeling becomes an automatic reaction to the sensation of a full stomach, the eating disorder victim will feel overwhelming shame and guilt at the very thought of eating. Hunger and guilt war within the person with an eating disorder with devastating consequences.

Creativity is stifled when one is afraid of making mistakes and exposing oneself to the opinions of others. Shame, like anger and fear, captures the attention and fixes it on the object or source of the fear, shame, or anger, creating a sort of tunnel vision. Creativity requires openness to ideas from different sources—a synthesis of previously unconnected elements. The tunnel vision of fear, shame, or anger can inhibit this aspect of creative thinking.

Chapter Four

Chronic shame causes many of us to create a "false self" for presentation to the world, and to hide many of our true feelings and wishes. While there may be plenty of times when it is appropriate to keep our feelings to ourselves, the consequent fear of revealing our "true selves" can be a serious trap. In a pernicious way, the mental act of choosing to hide tends to confirm the belief that we have a good reason to hide. The active response to the affect of shame tends to reinforce the circular process, deepening the shame. In many cases this results in difficulty asserting our wishes in perfectly appropriate ways. It can inhibit communication of our desires so much that we are left hoping someone will be sensitive enough to understand our needs without our having to express them ourselves.

Toxic Shame

When a shame response is reinforced by traumatic experience or repetition, such as repeated psychological, physical, or sexual abuse, it can lead to the formation of an emotional dynamic known as "toxic shame."

Toxic shame, its origins and its possible solutions will be discussed in detail in Chapter 6. It is mentioned here as one of the reasons why it is important to talk about and understand the affect of shame and its impact. The struggle to deal with the persistent pain of toxic shame can lead to complex behavior problems, including alcohol and drug abuse, eating disorders, depression, and suicidal impulses, as well as the severe erosion of self-esteem that accompanies each of these. The pain and confusion that a loved one experiences in his wish to help someone with a problem like alcoholism, an eating disorder, or chronic depression, contributes yet another layer of helplessness, shame, and anger to the family dynamics of those embroiled in toxic shame.

In short, it is clear that shame is associated with many of our most intractable problems in living together.

What is Shame?

Reconciliation

The release from shame and restoration to a healthy, honest, whole state of mind can come as reconciliation or restoration to full membership in the family or society. Another synonym for such restoration is recovery, as in recovery from an addiction or from an injury or illness. Reconciliation is part of the rhythm of everyday relationships. The scolded child must be reassured of his parents' continuing love in order to maintain healthy self-esteem. The pain caused by criticism must be forgiven in order for the friendship to survive. Trust must be restored in the marriage to allow a safe space for recovery from disappointments, betrayals, and failures.

The myths and sacred stories that have explored man's spiritual and emotional identity also point to reconciliation and redemption following a cleansing surrender. Joseph Campbell writes of the "hero's journey" common in mythology throughout history.[16] The hero must surrender to the mysterious forces of the universe before being able to triumph. This is a metaphor for the challenge facing each of us. We must be willing to let go of the shame-induced mask of the false self in order to be honest, whole, and free.

Chapter Five

The Shame-Anger Connection

The primary thesis of this book is that there is a necessary connection between the emotions of shame and anger that comes into play when we are criticized. I believe that this connection is hardwired in animals and human beings and can be shown to have survival value of its own, apart from the survival value of each of these affects separately.

The special link between the two can explain many observable behavioral phenomena in animals and humans and also account for some of the complex problems we have with shame and anger. For this reason it is important for us to look at the relationship between these two affects before we move on to dealing with these emotions in criticism situations.

From Surrender to Shame to Anger

As we have discussed, shame is the affect associated with surrender and defeat. It persists in our fundamental set of affects as a powerful basic emotion because it has survival value. If we remember that our basic emotions compel us to act immediately in ways that are most consistent with survival, the behaviors associated with shame begin to make sense. The defeated dog that slinks away after the fight is displaying the posture of shame, communicating surrender, and its abject posture may prevent it from being killed by its enemy. But this is only a temporary solution to the dangers of defeat. Shame alone does not have much sustainable survival value in a primitive environmental situation. The animal that continues to display the posture of shame and surrender is not going to get any respect from its peers, either at feeding time or in the competition for mating privileges. Soon after a defeat, the surviving loser is going to have to put on a renewed show of strength to establish some position in the hierarchy that determines who eats and who mates. Otherwise, it will be relegated to the lowest position in the pecking order, the least likely to survive in stressful circumstances.

Indeed, the phenomenon of the "pecking order" observed in most species, including our own, develops in response to the inhibiting effect of shame in the presence of a dominant member of the group. In the emotional jungle of elementary and middle school, some victims of bullies will react by wearing the facial expressions and posture of defeat a little bit too long. They are then at risk of becoming scapegoats—chronic victims—and of identifying themselves as victims who invite bullying. Most children, however, will need to prove their own worth by expressing anger and some aggressive action soon after their humiliation. It would seem appropriate that this anger and aggression be directed toward the bully, but this often isn't safe. So the aggression is generally taken out on another individual, usually a smaller or weaker one, either at school or at home.

Perhaps the inherent danger of sustained shame serves as an explanation for why shame is experienced by humans as such an intensely uncomfortable affect, often compared to a kind of death.

Chapter Five

Intolerable as an internal experience and unsustainable as a survival strategy, shame is always followed by a surge of aggression that helps the survivor reestablish a sense of power and position.

The aggression may be most easily expressed as a show of dominance toward another, probably a smaller or younger member of the group. The larger brother defeats and shames the younger one, who first retires, but soon reacts with a surge of aggression and seeks an even younger or smaller competitor to dominate. Thus surrender, defeat, and shame are universally followed by a surge of aggression or anger, though the defeated one may also learn to hide or redirect the anger if the expression of aggression holds dangers of its own.

The psychological truth of the shame-anger connection is powerfully portrayed in the biblical story of the first murder. In Genesis, Cain, the hard working farmer, is humiliated and shamed when God prefers the offering of his younger brother, Abel, the easy going shepherd. Cain complains to God and God warns him to 'beware of his anger,' for it may lead him to act sinfully. And, of course, in his rage, Cain kills Abel.

Our evolutionary emotional equipment dictates a surge of anger following the sting of shame whenever we perceive criticism as an attack. The experience of shame may have its evolutionary roots in life and death struggles, but it can be triggered in a young child by almost any scolding or rejection on the part of parents, older siblings, or other important figures in the child's life. The subsequent surge of aggression is also evident in the young child. If you speak sharply to a two-year-old, it is not unusual to see him cloud up in tears of shame and distress, then regroup and assault you with the worst insult in his vocabulary, or a pummeling of his little fist. Shame can often be evoked by a disappointment, a silent withholding of affection, a stern look, or a sharp word from a significant figure in the child's life. In the child's response, we see our evolutionary history in microcosm.

The young child, like the young lion cub wrestling with its siblings, experiments with a variety of outlets for its aggressive play. Through this process of trial and error, the young child and the young lion cub discover which of a variety of outlets works best. The child will also experiment with shorter or longer periods of withdrawal into the state of alienation characterized by shame.

Shame and Self-image

With the power of the imagination so well developed in the human brain, it is also possible for the young child to think about himself as an object of observation. This self-awareness begins to develop in children as early as age two. The child imagines himself in order to think about himself, and human imagination is a powerful and flexible tool. While the child cannot imagine containing two opposite emotions at the same time, he can imagine two self-images, one that is defeated and ashamed and one that is angry and strong. He can imagine the strong angry self acting powerfully in the world, fighting back against the sources of disappointment and humiliation. But another alternative the child can imagine is that of the strong angry self-image punishing the weaker, defeated, and ashamed self-image. This punishing aggressive self can become either a healthy conscience or harsh abusive superego. It can also grow into a harsh and unrealistic bully, constantly building its power by punishing its internal little brother.

As normal disappointments, scoldings, and criticisms repeatedly evoke shame and anger, each child experiments with various expressions of shame and anger according to the social situations in which he grows up.

It is understandable that we learn to associate criticism so closely with shame and anger and that it is almost impossible to perceive criticism as anything but an attack, or at the very least, a threat. The parent who is trying to be helpful with homework can accidentally trigger a painful avalanche of shame and anger without even a stern look or sharp word.

As the personality develops, an individual's shame response may grow to emphasize either the impulse to submit and surrender or the surge of aggression and anger that always follows the initial surrender. When shame is evoked as an automatic emotional response to criticism, we tend to respond in one of the two ways characteristic of shame. We may tend to accept the criticism without question and feel guilty or miserable. Or we may tend to reject the criticism without question and feel angry and defiant. Sometimes we bounce back and forth between the two.

Whether humiliation or anger dominates the response, the intense feelings evoked interfere with a calm and objective review of the situation.

Most of us learned our own personal styles of reacting to criticism when we were very young, when criticism was most often experienced as a scolding or teasing, and therefore became associated with shame. Since shame is always painful (and it is natural to want to avoid pain), early criticism, no matter how well intended or deserved, may soon lead to complex avoidance behaviors. So it is that some children learn to lie or blame others to avoid the pain of criticism. Other children learn to criticize themselves ruthlessly—partly to anticipate and avoid external criticism, and partly in hopes of reassurance from an external authority, such as a loving, forgiving parent. Early life is a constant process of negotiating relationships, bumping up against others, and triggering these powerful reactions in them and in ourselves. Fear, anger, shame, and joy can emerge in different combinations as we gradually memorize the complex patterns and sequences of events that are associated with each. We learn how to live in our community in this rough and tumble way.

It is neither possible nor desirable to eliminate the shame response entirely from the arena of criticism. Shame is the foundation for conscience and helps us remember the importance of other people's standards and expectations as well as our own. More often than not, however, an excessive shame response confuses the giving and accepting of criticism. So it is useful to learn methods of side-stepping the intense automatic shame response and cultivating a more detached and objective view of the perspective that the critic may provide.

The Shame-Anger Connection

Tracey grew up with a very self-critical mother. The phrase Tracey most associated with her mother was, "How could I have been so stupid!" She uttered this exasperated question whenever she made the smallest error or misstep, and sometimes abbreviated it to, "Stupid, Stupid, Stupid!" with a tight lipped expression of self-disdain. She would never think of calling Tracey stupid, even if Tracey had done something wrong, but sometimes when she was frustrated or impatient with her daughter, the same tight lipped expression told Tracey that her mother must have been thinking, "Stupid, Stupid, Stupid!" At an early age, Tracey began applying this epithet to herself, and although she knew she was smart, she slipped into the habit of angrily castigating herself for trivial errors as well as significant ones. Over the years, the habit of repeating this self-castigation in moments of frustration became a part of the way she thought about herself, part of her own identity.

Geoff grew up with parents who were self-confident and very supportive. Though not immune to the frustrations of family life, Geoff's father was able to shrug off small catastrophes fairly quickly. He liked to say, "Everyone makes mistakes. The important thing is to learn from them." When Geoff became frustrated with something and angry with himself, his father usually sat down with him and patiently helped him find a solution—not doing it for the boy, but asking the right questions and encouraging him. When the problem was solved, his father always congratulated Geoff quite naturally on the solution. Thus Geoff began to learn that a mistake was not just a shameful failure, but could also be an opportunity for creative problem solving. If anger and blame could be set aside and patience and curiosity applied, the outlook was good. Frequent repetition of this approach to problems caused it to become a part of Geoff's view of the world and of himself, part of his resilient and confident identity.

Shame and Self-worth: The Problem of "Deserving"

One of the concepts that we form in response to social training is the idea that we deserve good things as rewards for "good" behavior, or, because of "bad" behavior, we do not deserve good things. This is reinforced by many repetitions of punishments in which something desirable is withheld as a punishment or given as a reward for compliant behavior. Such rewards and punishments are not in and of themselves destructive, but they reinforce a concept that is deeply embedded in the language of many, but not all, cultures. As the child learns the language of his culture while negotiating the behavioral learning emotionally charged with shame and anger, the concepts of deserving or self-worth become charged with the emotional power of shame and anger.

Descriptions of the staunchly Calvinist morality of 18th Century Scotland in Iain Pears' novel The Portrait[17] highlight the cultural training that surrounds the protagonist in his early years and leave him with a ruthlessly judgmental attitude toward himself and others. In this portrayal of one culture, self-aggrandizement is sinful and vicious self-criticism is expected.

By contrast, in traditional Tibetan culture, individual shame is an alien concept. I do not think it is because Tibetans are hardwired differently, but because they are trained in the Buddhist belief that desire and ego are distractions from the truth and should be gently set aside. Individuals who are more successful at quelling ambition and fear, at subjugating the ego, are considered blessed, and the highest achievers in this respect are also the most humble.

As a child learns her culture's concepts of individuals being deserving or undeserving, she comes to view herself in one category or the other. The underlying belief that I deserve good things or don't deserve good things becomes memorized along with the other conclusions or lessons of early life. An adult with talent and accomplishments aplenty can be troubled by a nagging feeling that he does not deserve the good things in life, even when he has worked hard for them. Alternatively, some children are raised in an environment of entitlement which teaches them that they deserve anything good that happens. This can lead to a strong sense of self-confidence, but it can also lead to an arrogant expectation of honor and success without much personal effort.

The Shame-Anger Connection

Awareness of cultural elements that impact on one's sense of self-worth, and of the interplay of shame and anger with these cultural elements in the early years can help balance any exaggerated tendency toward very high or very low self-worth that might lead to problems.

Releasing Shame with Reconciliation

When the emotional state of shame is relieved or ended by some change of circumstances, or perhaps by the passage of time following the event that triggered shame, affect theorists say that the shame is released. The shamed animal that finds the energy to reassert itself is freed of the emotional burden or shackles of shame and assumes a normal emotional posture in the world or community in which it lives. The scolded child who is comforted and reassured of his parents' continued affection resumes a sense of safety and confidence in his position in the world represented by his family.

As we have discussed, when an animal is defeated in competition and withdraws from the field for a while it must eventually find a way to reenter the pecking order to release the shame. Most often, this involves confronting another animal and winning a position in the hierarchy that determines who eats and mates first, and who controls what territory.

Young animals practice their hunting and fighting skills through playful combat with siblings and parents. You can watch the tiger cubs at the zoo "ambushing" their mother. The attacks are quickly shrugged off unless the mother tiger is feeling tired or irritable. The cubs withdraw briefly before attempting their next assault. Sometimes, they will give up on attacking mother for a while and attack one another. These playful attacks are cheerfully tolerated for the most part and there is no shaming defeat when the attacks fail.

Similar playful attacks are enacted by human children upon their parents and siblings. Most of the time, parents will tolerate these attacks patiently, sometimes even initiating gentle roughhousing. Siblings may not be so patient and sometimes parents' patience for this is stretched thin and a sharp response sends the child away tearfully. Many times, when the child signals her distress over the rebuke, the parent will reach out with soothing affection. This expression of affection and reassurance creates an opportunity for reconciliation between parent and child or between siblings that also releases shame. The child no longer feels shamed, defeated, or exiled, but now feels comforted, welcomed, and reassured. **The sense of safety and acceptance that is possible as a result of parental soothing after a shaming event is crucial to self-esteem, so parents' awareness of the importance of reconciliation is essential**.

Because we have long memories for emotionally charged events, significant problems can be generated by shame and anger in our early years if they are left unreconciled. The importance of reconciliation as an antidote to shame will be seen in the context of the significant problems of toxic shame and depression as we explore them in the following chapters.

Chapter Six
Toxic Shame

Julie was an attractive, intelligent, and apparently healthy young woman who suffered secretly from toxic shame. Despite the positive feedback from others regarding her appearance, her generosity, her hard work and productivity, she was flooded with horror that others would discover the world of ugliness, sloth, incompetence, and selfishness that she believed to be the truth about herself. This "truth" was based on what she heard from a cruel and angry inner judge constantly responding to runaway shame. Because her shame would be magnified if exposed to others, she was terrified that her secret would be discovered. The possibility of discovery was so horrifying and disgusting that she could not ignore the danger of it or cease searching for evidence of it. She searched in the mirror for every bulge or fold of skin that might be evidence of fat. She reviewed her behavior for mistakes or omissions and savagely criticized the faults she thought she could see. Her intense shame over her perceived failure and her immediate anger at

Chapter Six

herself kept her in an exhausted emotional state, and she resorted to desperate behaviors to relieve the pressure. Rigidly defined dieting gave her a sense of control over some of the runaway shame. But when intense hunger drove her to eat more than she allowed herself, she was again flooded with shame and anxiety and resorted to vomiting. Since most people she knew were repulsed by intentional vomiting, shame surged back with an added dose of disgust (easily associated with vomiting) and angry self-contempt. She began to seek relief from the inner pain and self-contempt through a self-punishing ritual of cutting herself superficially but painfully. The physical pain was a distraction from the emotional pain. It generated a release of endorphins (brain chemicals that kick in as a response to shock and pain) that helped dull both physical and emotional pain. This gave her a sense of control over the imminent shaming exposure and external punishment she anticipated in her imagination. But the secretiveness of the purging and the cutting further isolated her from others, leaving her alone with an imagination dominated by a combination of shame and anger that seemed increasingly real and inevitable.

To many readers, Julie's situation and her responses may seem an unbelievable exaggeration. But it is an all too familiar story to counselors working with young people struggling with eating disorders or addictions. For these counselors, toxic shame is a well-recognized concept. Alcohol or drugs may seem to offer quick and easy relief for shame and anger, especially for adolescents whose shame and anger may cut them off from potential sources of healthy adult or peer support. But the secrecy of an eating disorder, or of illegal drugs or alcohol abuse, and the consequences of their impact on performance and relationships soon adds to the accumulating burden of shame and anger, creating an incubator for the hatred of self and others that comes from toxic shame.

Kaufman writes: "Shame is the affect which is the source of many complex and disturbing inner states: depression, alienation, self-doubt, isolating loneliness, paranoid and schizoid phenomena, compulsive disorders, splitting of the self, perfectionism, a deep sense of inferiority, inadequacy or failure,

Toxic Shame

the so-called borderline conditions, and disorders of narcissism."[18]

Healthy shame contributes to the child's sense of limits, the conscience by which he learns to regulate his impulses in order to fit in with the family and the world. But the development of a healthy conscience is a subtle pattern that can only develop in the context of a fair balance between consistent, firm limit setting (even though this triggers a shame response for the child) and loving reassurance and acceptance. Erik Erikson, author of Childhood and Society, writes of the developmental task of striking a balance between autonomy and shame at 15 months when children begin to experiment with letting go of parents and saying no.[19]

Erikson believes that a child at this age needs firmness, consistency, and caring so that she is reassured that the interpersonal bridge between herself and the caretaker is not broken when limits are set. The balance between scolding and the reassurance of continuing love is necessary for developing healthy shame as contrasted with toxic shame. When the child is scolded, he is temporarily cast out of the good graces of the parent or caretaker on whom he depends. The sting of this loss of affection, even if it is very brief, is a powerful motivator for the child to accept the limits the caretaker is setting. When he does accept the limits and demonstrates some remorse or understanding and perhaps a desire to do better next time, he is accepted back into the loving embrace of the caretaker and the distress of censure is relieved but not forgotten. The memory of the pain remains as a powerful reminder of the limits that must be respected.

The shame response develops in a healthy way when the caretaker is consistent, the shaming not too intense or lengthy, and the reconciliation follows promptly upon the child's contrition. But despite the best intentions of loving parents, many children seem to experience and expect excessive shame and do not learn to trust in the likelihood of loving reconciliation. Sometimes the caretaker is punitive or abusive. Sometimes the failure of the caretaker to adequately demonstrate forgiveness or reassurance is enough to upset the

Chapter Six

balance of shame and reconciliation and leave the child in an outcast state long enough to plant a seed of toxic shame.

The most powerful ability of the human mind is imagination: the ability to combine or distort images, memories, and feelings from past experience to make up new mental constructs, many of which can be thought of as future possibilities. When an emotion is associated with an imagined future possibility, the individual is motivated to act to achieve that possibility (if it is desirable) or to avoid it (if it is painful or undesirable). Because we can imagine the shame of rejection, censure, or punishment associated with misbehavior, we are motivated to behave. This is the foundation of our conscience.

For an adult with long established emotional habits, learning to quiet a simple, relatively healthy, but overactive shame response is challenging enough. We will discuss methods of quieting shame and anger in Chapter 8. Dealing with "toxic shame" is another order of magnitude.

Toxic shame is a complex learned response pattern. This pattern can develop when the powerful ability of the imagination acts upon certain combinations of shame and anger in such a way as to reinforce them in an escalating cycle. Because of the flexibility of our big brains, we have the ability to imagine many future possibilities and associate feelings with them that inspire in us excitement, fear, anger, disgust, or any of the range of emotions familiar to us at any level of intensity. If an individual's life experience has made it easy for him to imagine a lot of future scenes that evoke intense shame, fear, or anger, it is possible to populate the future with almost unlimited opportunities for more shame, fear, and anger. As the individual anticipates more and more shame and anger scattered everywhere among future possibilities the escalating cycle of shame runs out of control. Toxic shame becomes a kind of self-generating emotional torture that smothers healthy options and motivates the individual to escape at any cost. Some of us create this troubling tapestry by trial and error, with many repetitions in imagination and in real experience. After so many repetitions, we have accidentally memorized an emotional response pattern that then becomes automatic and seems

Toxic Shame

inevitable. How does toxic shame get started? And what can we do about it?

Abuse as a Cause of Toxic Shame

Toxic shame is a fairly predictable learned response when a child is abused or repeatedly hurt early in life and finds no safe source of comfort or protection. When a child is hurt or abused, she will naturally seek comfort or protection unless prevented from doing so. Sometimes she is prevented by the threats of the abuser or by her own fear of the consequences of talking about the abuse. Sometimes when she seeks comfort, she may be ignored, disbelieved, scolded for talking about unacceptable things, or even accused of lying.

The following quote from one of the contributors to The Shame Project, a collection of shame experiences created by the staff of the Center for Pastoral Counseling of Virginia, gives us an example of a child who feels blamed for her own misfortune.

> "My struggle with shame began with my father telling me that I was the cause for his emotionless cruelty and his leaving our family. I was left with my mother and my sister. My mentally ill sister tried often to kill me along with her own self-destruction. My mother, living her own serial shame, told me I was responsible for making up for everyone else's failure... including myself when I inevitably failed her, as well. This led me to believe as a first principle that those who should most naturally and simply love me were excused from that burden. I did not expect to be loved by members of my nuclear family, and this was transferred to all others I might fall in love with. They wouldn't or shouldn't love me either... unless I performed heroic feats in complex sagas of engineered perfection in service to them."[20]

The failure to find protection leaves the child no choice but to hide the hurt, and she generally interprets this to mean that the hurting is somehow her fault. The hurt must have happened because she was bad in some way.

51

Chapter Six

Children often conclude that they are bad when adults do not like the normal noisiness or messiness that goes along with healthy play. This is a common mistake in the formation of conscience. When adult irritation emerges in response to the child seeking comfort, she can conclude that needing comfort is bad and learn to associate shame or fear with normal needs.

An abusive situation generates many repetitions of this dilemma and much shame about needing or wanting comfort. If the abuse is sexual, shame about sexuality takes root in this kind of experience and the child's struggle to make sense of it. Secret shame about sexual abuse can remain dormant until preadolescent or adolescent development precipitates a new challenge. When the young person's emerging sexual drives or social competitiveness awakens the secret shame associated with abuse at a time when her self-definition is the central psychological task, this churning shame and frustration can quickly create a cyclone of intense feelings feeding the toxic shame cycle. At this point, if the original abuse has never been discussed and comfort has never been sought or given, it is very difficult for the young person to recognize the mistake in her assumptions about herself.

Other Potential Causes

Although abusive environments are most likely to generate the toxic shame syndrome, it can develop in response to less virulent stimuli. Children need to be acknowledged and listened to; they need to have their fears and pains comforted, even if they are normal childish fears and pains. When a parent is too much absent, or too depressed or anxious, or too intoxicated, or too impaired or stressed and frustrated to respond to a child's needs, the effect is similar to that of the abused child who is not protected. At some level the child concludes, "I hurt, but no one cares, so I must not be worth caring about." The precipitating hurt may not be as intense as abuse, but the conclusion that the child draws is the same, and may be repeated many times. In some families, the frustration may be passed from one sibling to another, with one child in the family getting the accumulated frustrations of others, because there is too little comfort and acknowledgement to go around.

The metaphor of a mental filing cabinet may help us to better understand how toxic shame can develop. Memories are stored in the mind according to the emotion with which they are associated. The stronger the emotion, the more likely this is. Using the filing cabinet metaphor, one can imagine that memories of fearful experiences are stored together in one drawer, anger memories are stored together in another, and startle or shock memories are stored close to fear and anger. Joyful or sad memories are stored farther away. In all these drawers, the memories associated with the most powerful emotional charges tend to be stored near the front of the file drawer and are most easily accessed. When anger is triggered, the anger file drawer opens, and we can easily access a collection of remembered anger experiences stored there. Perhaps this facilitates problem solving in a crisis by quickly bringing to mind similar experiences, but remembering these experiences also tends to intensify the anger and subtly encourages us to search further in the same file drawer.

Furthermore, opening one drawer in the mental filing cabinet tends to affect access to other drawers. Some drawers are connected, while others are mutually exclusive. Opening the anger file drawer may also lead to memories associated with fear, but not to joy and love. Because the affects of fear and anger arouse us to action and the affects of joy and love trigger relaxation, these affects, and the memories associated with them are mutually exclusive. Anger interferes with love, and love or joy tempers or interferes with anger. This is not to say that you can't be angry with someone you love, but that at the moment you are angry, the feelings of love cannot be experienced in the same way.

Recent brain research shows that the memories associated with emergency problem solving and with the affects of fear, anger, and shame, tend to be processed in an area of the brain known as the right prefrontal lobe (of the cerebral cortex). Interestingly, the memories associated with the emotions of love, joy, and compassion are processed in the left prefrontal lobe. Related research has shown that monks with considerable training in meditation on compassion have shown very high levels of activity in the left prefrontal lobe. Many of us, however, spend a great deal of time problem solving in the right prefrontal lobe. Unfortunately, memories associated with calm confidence, joyful excitement, or creativity (left prefrontal lobe) are usually hidden when the anger drawer is open in the right prefrontal lobe. Persons who are depressed often find it difficult to remember when they were happy, and when their depression has passed, they often find it difficult to remember how depressed they were only a few weeks ago.

The longer the anger file drawer is open and the more anger memories are reviewed, the more intense the anger becomes, until acting on the anger is irresistible. When action is taken, or even vividly imagined, a new memory is formed and stored in the anger file drawer, which is soon filled with intense anger memories that pop up quickly in response to any stimulus for anger. In addition to this, it is important to note that the brain appears to be designed to pay attention to fear, pain, and anger first—probably because these are critical emotions associated with dangerous survival situations. This can cause us to go to these memory drawers more often and spend more time with them, thus leading to emotional habits or chain reactions.

If all the memories associated with shame are stored in the same drawer of the mental filing cabinet, and a child has many opportunities to visit and revisit that drawer triggered by new experiences of shame or reminders of past experiences, the child begins to find access to those memories becoming more and more common and automatic. It is as if each time the drawer is opened, it opens more easily, and reviewing those painful memories is almost as painful as experiencing them the first time. Post traumatic stress disorder is characterized by vivid painful memories of an intensely painful experience, often triggered by an inadvertent reminder.

Experience alone is not the only factor contributing to the development of increased sensitivity to one emotion or another. Some children are born more anxious than others and may be more likely to experience life through a filter of anxiety. The same could be true for the affect of shame. Some children are innately predisposed to feel shame, so it may be easier for life experiences to reinforce that predisposition. Whatever the precipitating circumstances, the child's imagination can provide plenty of material to elaborate on basic dangers and increase the need for comfort. The child's imagination is also a source of hypotheses for why comfort remains elusive as the child tries to understand why she has to endure fear and shame.

Sometimes adults provide explanations for the child's pain by stating, vaguely or specifically, that she deserves to feel bad because she has been bad in some way. This is such a common experience that many adults (having survived the same treatment in their own childhoods) do not recognize how insidiously this contributes to the child's belief in her own worthlessness. The child, knowing better than to argue back, learns to punish or criticize herself for being "bad," and the seeds of toxic shame are sown. Shame and anger, paired in the dance of self-criticism, find fertile fields in the child's imagination and can grow into grotesque webs of damaged self-esteem.

Perfectionism

For a certain percentage of children who are shamed directly or indirectly, but also experience praise and success in the eyes of others, there is the trap of perfectionism. Perfectionism is based on the assumption that one can avoid shame and criticism if only one can eliminate all flaws and achieve the state of perfection beyond all possible criticism. It is logically obvious that perfection is an impossible goal, and the futility of this hope is easily observable from a brief survey of tabloid newspapers that routinely ridicule our most admired and successful celebrities. However, the magical assumption of underlying perfectionism has nothing to do with logic or experience. Efforts toward perfection are driven by the fear of anticipated criticism and spurred on by a relentless inner critic who knows all of our own secret flaws and failures, however invisible these may be to others. The discipline of perfectionism dictates that each new level of achievement or success becomes the minimum acceptable standard to avoid disappointment and shame. Since this tyrannical standard cannot be met, the individual experiences constant self-shaming and anticipation of shame. Shame avoidance through ever more arduous efforts becomes a way of life, and fear of failure becomes a constant companion. Sometimes the fear of failure is translated into fear of fat, fear of looking stupid, or fear of being alone.

The cumulative stress of perfectionism leads to mistakes, physical symptoms, and burnout. The highly accomplished perfectionist individual may become the target of attacks from jealous rivals, creating additional stress. The anger that follows closely on the heels of all this shame and anxiety can be directed primarily at the self. But sometimes the anger overflows onto innocent others with the result that the perfectionist then feels guilty about her own perfection-driven anger. A blast of self-punishing anger then follows immediately and the spiral of toxic shame continues.

Other Reinforcers for Shame

We live in a society in which shaming and blaming are common occurrences. We're not unique in this. In fact there may be only a few instances in human history where shame and blame have not been dominant social themes. Shame plays a role in establishing the social pecking order that structures our societies. Children are exposed to societal shame both directly and indirectly. Direct exposure comes on the playground or in the sibling group, where peers and older children struggle for identity, power, and acceptance by teasing or bullying. Teasers and bullies may imitate the words, tones, and facial expressions of their parents, older siblings, TV heroes, or other role models whom they have witnessed engaging in shaming behaviors.

When a child is subjected to a continual barrage of harsh criticism based on unclear or impossible expectations, there is no way he can escape the impact of shame by learning to adapt to the critic's or the society's values or expectations. The result is that the child learns a pattern of toxic shame in response to any social contact, and internalizes an identity of failure and inadequacy. Adults can also be traumatized by a sustained and punishing assault of vicious criticism that amounts to emotional bullying.

The victims of teasing and bullying must endure a certain amount of shame and find a way to neutralize it, or they are at risk of internalizing it as a seed that can grow into toxic shame. Many children find relief in passing on the pain by teasing another child in the eternal chain of power struggles involved in establishing social position in groups. Others find comfort from parents or friends to undo the shame of teasing or bullying through reconciliation. For some, repeated victimization is not resolved, and in order to make sense of the recurring pain, the child forms an assumption about himself as inferior, deserving of abuse, and fated to be an outsider. He hides his vulnerability as best he can, but is always acutely aware of the potential danger of exposure. Such constant vigilance provides another opportunity for the development of toxic shame.

Children can also be exposed to shame indirectly, by virtue of their natural empathy, when they witness shaming of others close to them. If Joey sees his older brother painfully shamed or victimized and is powerless to do anything about it, he may feel the pain of shame and helplessness through his empathic identification with his brother. This is the position of the child who witnesses abuse in his family but is not the direct victim of the abuse. A combination of the impact of shame and fear along with a sense of powerlessness to protect the victim can lead to a desperate need to balance and make sense of the powerful warring feelings within.

John, a man in his fifties, sought counseling for problems of anxiety when flying. In the family history, he revealed that he (along with all of his 5 sisters) had been treated abusively by his father—who later abandoned the family. As the only boy in the family, he was given special status and approval by his maternal grandfather, but always felt guilty about this special position. When he learned, in his 20's, that each of his sisters had been molested by the same maternal grandfather, he was so flooded with guilt and rage that he had to repress it in order to function. Although he himself had not been violated by the grandfather, his feelings of helplessness as a member of the family were intolerable and generated so much distress that they found expression in grim ambition, irritability, and anxiety. Talking about the family history released a flood of shame and anger that he eventually realized he had been suppressing for years. The stress of all this secret shame and anger had the result of making him an angry and critical father. As he continued his counseling, he reported that his wife was describing dramatic changes in his behavior at home and his 7 year old son was becoming less fearful of him. Though working through all of the deeply buried shame and anger took years to complete, the benefits began to show up relatively early on and were steadily consolidated.

While John was working through his own family history of abuse, his young son was molested by a neighborhood bully. John was able to seek therapy for his son and protect him by helping in the prosecution of the perpetrator. After a year of play therapy, and with sensitive support by John and his wife, the boy made an excellent recovery and symptoms of poor performance in school and oppositional tantrums at home disappeared.

John believed that his own resolution of the toxic shame of his family history enabled him to support his son through a similar crisis. Because of his resolution of the shame, he was able to face, and eventually resolve, the feelings of helplessness and rage triggered by his son's victimization.

The phenomenon of indirect shame can also be observed in some children whose parents fight bitterly. The child may identify with one parent and feel indirectly shamed or attacked or may simply feel powerless to prevent the chaos and the danger that his family will be destroyed. Powerlessness evokes feelings of shame and futile anger that can easily be redirected against the self.

These examples demonstrate how the triggers for shame can multiply as the internal dance of shame and anger plays out. A real traumatic experience evokes shame, then anticipation of shame evokes more shame, shame evokes anger, anger is expressed in a manner that creates more problems, ultimately leading to more shame and anger. The individual feels a loss of control over personal feelings and reactions: more shame and anger at one's self. The individual hides the shame, and the knowledge of the secret fault evokes more shame. A vortex of self-loathing is generated that can be literally life threatening.

Healing Toxic Shame

Releasing the accumulated toxic shame of many years and interrupting a well established pattern of self-shaming are delicate and demanding tasks. Because shame compels us to hide, self-exposure in the search for healing feels extremely dangerous. Courage, patience, and persistence are required, and a trusting relationship with a counselor or compassionate support group are necessary. Someone has to provide an alternative to the ruthless inner voice of self-criticism.

The Courage to Heal, by Bass and Davis, Letting Go of Shame, by Potter-Efron, and Bradshaw's classic Healing the Shame that Binds You are excellent books that outline the complex process of healing toxic shame. Each encourages the individual to seek a therapeutic ally he can trust, and to be patient and cautious in challenging the demons of shame. Urgent or impulsive efforts to change can easily backfire when unrealistic expectations lead to disappointments that are interpreted as failures and become more grounds for shame and hopelessness. The choice of a therapeutic ally, whether an individual counselor or a group, must be carefully made. It is essential that the counselor or group members understand and respect the destructive power of toxic shame.

In the next chapter, we will explore how toxic shame is related to the most common of our mental health complaints: depression. Researchers tell us that 10% of Americans are depressed at any one point in time and that 25% report having experienced depression at some time in their lives.

Chapter Seven

Shame, Anger, and Depression

Emotional states can be seen as either normal or pathological depending upon the degree of intensity in relation to the circumstances. For example, anger is a normal adaptive response in some situations, but excessive rage, inappropriate to the circumstances, is abnormal. Rage can be the primary symptomatic criteria for a number of nervous and mental disorders delineated in the Diagnostic and Statistical Manual (DSM) that defines mental illnesses for medical professionals.[21] Fear is also a normal and adaptive emotional response in many situations, but chronic or severe anxiety, panic attacks, and disabling phobias, all related to the basic emotion of fear, are defined as illnesses in the DSM.

There has been a long debate among psychologists and philosophers as to whether depression, which is itself a term for a whole category of mood disorders in the DSM, is an illness or a normal response to overwhelming circumstances.

Shame, Anger, and Depression

My sense is that the emotional phenomena, and they are plural, that we call depression can be either or both. Depression may be experienced as a normal response to some situations such as grief or catastrophe, but when it is prolonged, severe, or disabling, we can consider it an illness.

Modern psychopharmacology tends to leave us with the impression that depression is the result of faulty brain chemistry, correctable by medications such as Prozac or Wellbutrin. The popularity of this treatment has led some to argue that we may be chemically modifying normal emotional states and that this could have unintended consequences. Even when medications provide effective relief from depression, this approach is not as simple as we would like to think. Side effects and differing responses to medication make the job of the psychopharmacologist more complex than we might wish.

Before the advent of antidepressants, psychoanalysts and psychologists proposed a variety of explanations for the clinical phenomenon of depression, or "melancholia" as it was called in earlier times. Until recently, most of the psychological explanations relied on a theory of a "self-destructive impulse" in our natures or anger turned toward the self to explain depression. The proliferation of explanations for depression has led to a variety of treatment approaches, with inconsistent results, based on these various theories.

Throughout our discussion of shame and anger, we have been exploring affective or emotional responses in terms of evolutionary psychology. If we look at our emotions through the lens of evolutionary advantage, we have to ask whether there is a possible survival value for them in evolutionary terms. It is easy to understand the survival value of fear and anger as we have discussed before. In Chapter 4, we explored the possible evolutionary survival value of shame. Is it possible that depression can be seen as having survival value as well?

Rank Theory

One theory for the evolutionary advantage of depression is known as rank theory. In their book, Evolutionary Psychiatry,

Chapter Seven

Anthony Stevens and John Price describe "rank theory" and its implications for depression as follows:

> "...rank theory proposes that depression is an adaptive response to losing rank and conceiving of oneself as a loser. The adaptive function of the depression, according to rank theory, is to facilitate losing and to promote accommodation to the fact that one has lost. In other words, the depressive state evolved to promote the acceptance of the subordinate role and the loss of resources which can only be secured by holding higher rank in the dominance hierarchy. The function of this depressive adaptation is to prevent the loser in a status conflict from suffering further injury and to preserve the stability and competitive efficiency of the group by maintaining social homeostasis. In circumstances of defeat and enforced subordination, an internal inhibitory process comes into operation which causes the individual to cease competing and reduce his level of aspiration. This inhibitory process is *involuntary* and results in the loss of energy, depressed mood, sleep disturbance, poor appetite, retarded movements, and loss of confidence which are typical characteristics of depression. One important contribution of rank theory is that it proposes a hypothesis of how depression actually evolved: it emerged as the *yielding* component of ritual agonistic conflict. This has been called the **yielding subroutine** (Price and Sloman, 1987). The adaptive function of the yielding subroutine is twofold: first, it ensures that the yielder truly yields and does not attempt to make a comeback, and, second, the yielder reassures the winner that yielding has truly taken place, so that the conflict ends, with no further damage to the yielder. Relative social harmony is then restored."[22]

Rank theory so closely parallels our explanation of the evolutionary advantage of shame that it suggests that shame

Shame, Anger, and Depression

and depression may have the same evolutionary roots. This reinforces the association between depression and various manifestations of shame. Affect theorists argue that the basic affect of shame can manifest as embarrassment, shyness, low self-esteem, or guilt, depending on the circumstances triggering it. Depression is often associated with low self-esteem, a vague or excessive sense of guilt, social withdrawal or isolation similar to shyness, and a sense of powerlessness or hopelessness similar to the conditions of defeat. The strong connection between the affect of shame and the more complex phenomena of depression allows for speculation regarding the psychological and evolutionary relationship between the two. Can persistent shaming experiences lead to depression? Does a clinical depression triggered by brain chemistry usually evoke the shame response (both feelings of helplessness and anger are characteristic of depression)?

The Abandonment Response

The emotional state we refer to as depression also has many similarities with another emotion, the one we think of as loneliness, but may more appropriately be called the "abandonment response." The abandonment response has its roots in an affect that has critical survival value for babies and newborn animals. The sense of sadness and despair a small child or animal feels on being left alone is painful and elicits two kinds of behavior. First the baby cries, which has the potential to get Mom's attention in case she has wandered off and misplaced the baby. Have you ever heard the plaintive sound of a bear cub or elephant calf separated from its mother? It is not difficult to recognize the tone of fear and sadness in the sound of their cries. If the mother is unable to or does not respond to this cry, the baby will eventually fall into a quiet state of despair and depression. Even this emotional state has survival value. For an infant separated from its mother, continued crying could attract the attention of a predator. Falling into a state of depression is the only option available to the infant to conserve its energy and give the mother time to sniff it out and come to the rescue.

Chapter Seven

Human infants that are not stimulated by cuddling and eye contact with a nurturing caretaker also fall into this state of energy conservation. It is referred to as "anaclitic depression" and is observed in orphans in institutions where there is inadequate attention to the infants. It is well understood now that human babies' brains stop developing in this state. They fail to thrive and may die even if they are offered adequate nourishment.

Even a brief exposure to the experience of abandonment is enough to trigger some of the emotional response that we later associate with loneliness or despair. Almost all of us have had some taste of the affect of helplessness and anguish associated with the experience of abandonment, however brief and unintended. A good percentage of children have experienced enough abandonment to have memories of the intense, prolonged despair and helplessness that is the earliest precursor of anaclitic depression. Whether or not one's life experience has triggered the emotion, it may well be that we all come equipped to respond to abandonment in this way if it happens to us. We have the capacity for a depression response, or an abandonment response, to get us through the earliest months of life until we have more resources to help ourselves in a pinch. But what happens to the capacity for an important emotional response when we no longer need it? When we are old enough to take care of ourselves, does the capacity for depression (the abandonment response) disappear?

Because this state of despair and depression is so painful, it is easily remembered and associated with reminders of abandonment. So when we experience a reminder of abandonment later in life, it is natural to recreate the pain of depression associated with abandonment, and this is the experience we call loneliness. Reminders of abandonment can be subtle, such as scenes in a movie where a character is experiencing loneliness. Or they can be the natural reaction to the loss of an important person in your life.

They can also be triggered by imagined future experiences of abandonment and solitude. Some depressed individuals are so completely convinced of the hopelessness of their future that they are unable to take any comfort in current companionship. They live in the future of anticipated loneliness.

As we discussed in the last chapter, memories of emotional experiences are associated as if they are stored together in a mental filing cabinet with drawers assigned to different emotional states. Memories of the powerful feeling of helplessness and abandonment are stored together in the same way as memories associated with fear or anger. If a young person has a lot of abandonment experiences, or a lot of experiences of losing, or other experiences associated with the feelings of loneliness, helplessness, and despair, the mind will have a drawer full of memories that evoke this emotion. The pathway to that drawer may be better worn than the pathway to other drawers, so circumstances that are in any way similar may evoke the feeling, and the drawer becomes stuffed with associated memories and is easier to access. This can result in a young person beginning to formulate an understanding of their world and their life centered on the feelings of abandonment and despair. One can learn to expect this kind of experience and, anticipating it, evoke the feeling even in circumstances where it is not really necessary or appropriate. Thus we can have the experience of feeling lonely in a room full of familiar faces, because something has taken us to the mental file drawer stuffed with reminders of abandonment.

Anger and Depression

The surrender response we have discussed as an evolutionary explanation for the affect of shame is similar to the "yielding subroutine" described by Stevens and Price in their exploration of rank theory of depression. But Stevens and Price do not posit an anger or aggression response following the surrender experience, though anger is frequently experienced as a part of depression. In psychoanalytic theory and other contemporary schools of psychology, anger is recognized as a common—almost universal—component of depression. Irritability is one of the symptoms of depression delineated in the DSM, and anger toward the self is often experienced as part of depression.

One way to explain how all of these concepts might fit together is to hypothesize that the shame/anger response can be triggered by a variety of events other than those typically associated with defeat or humiliation. It may be that a change in brain chemistry caused by poor nutrition, fatigue, or illness triggers an affect or feeling similar to defeat and evokes the shame/anger response. The radical hormonal changes following childbirth can trigger a state known as post partum depression in many women. It may be that a major loss or disappointment triggers a feeling response so similar to defeat that shame and anger are evoked. Or it may be that a new event reminds the individual of past events so traumatic or so painful that the shame/anger response is evoked.

Whatever the cause, when shame and anger are evoked, anger at oneself is a common response. Expressing anger toward the self, in thought or action, is a mental activity that results in a lose-lose situation. The person who is angry at himself is in a bind. Either he is right to think he is a loser or he is crazy, confused, deluded, or otherwise wrong to think it. Though no one would consciously choose to place himself in a lose-lose trap like this, once you stumble into it, it can be difficult to see a way out.

Shame and anger at oneself, if experienced often, is a routine that becomes familiar—the brain responds to a variety of triggers with shame and anger, and depression becomes more likely. Recent reports of studies of pain indicate that when newborn infants are exposed to a series of painful procedures, they are more sensitive to pain later in life. It is as if the developing brain of the infant learns to pay attention to pain as a primary experience and gives it more attention in the future. Similarly, infants who are stressed, ignored, or disappointed early in life may learn the "yielding subroutine" of shame and anger early on and give it a more prominent place in their repertoire of choices later in life, practicing it unintentionally until it becomes a familiar "default" response to life situations.

Shame, Anger, and Depression

Why don't we all become obsessed with abandonment?

If it is so easy to fill a mental file drawer with fear, anger, loneliness, or shame, how does it happen that we are not all depressed, phobic rage-aholics? For an answer to this question, we look again to evolutionary psychology and to what we know about mind-body interaction.

In addition to the emergency response emotions of fear, anger, shame, and some related ones such as surprise, excitement, and distress, we also come hardwired for the emotional states of contentment and joy. There is an entire component of the nervous system geared to arousal in case of need for quick response. This is called the "sympathetic nervous system," which is central to the fight/flight response. But there is another component geared to relaxation and pleasure called the "parasympathetic nervous system." If it were not for the parasympathetic nervous system, we would have no way to relax, and we would burn out from stress in short order. Anger, fear, and excitement are physically demanding emotions. They are designed for short term emergency response and lead to a rise in blood pressure, muscle tension, and an increase in cholesterol, all of which create health problems if they become chronic instead of acute or short term responses. This is why the Type A personality who is always ready for the next deadline is more vulnerable to coronary artery disease, and why chronically stressed individuals are prone to headaches and backaches.[23] But because we come equipped with an automatic relaxation response we are able to relax once the emergency has passed. Unfortunately, many of us learn to override our relaxation response and keep ourselves in a constant state of readiness for emergency. We are not hardwired to worry all the time, but we can learn to do this, and our fast paced, achievement oriented, high tech cultural environment provide both the incentive and the training to become full time worriers.

Early in life we learn to anticipate problems in the hope of solving them or at least preparing ourselves for them. We imagine the problem situation in the future and feel some anticipatory anxiety as we zoom in on it in our mind's eye. If the problem occurs later, we can say, "I was right to worry about that." And if the problem doesn't occur later or we solve or avoid it, we can say, "Worrying helped me avoid that problem." We may even believe that the worrying helped in some magical way when nothing at all was done to solve or avoid the problem!

One of the problems we frequently face is not getting something done on time. In our fast paced, technologically advanced culture, we expect to do more and more in less and less time, giving us more and more to worry about. Some psychologists have suggested that the wealth of activities available to middle class children these days actually leads to higher expectations, as well as demands on the child's time. Therefore, even children must deal with the stress of our high expectations and busy lifestyles.

Synaptic connections are forged between nerve cells (neurons) in the brain to connect a perceived stimulus and the emotional and cognitive responses to that stimulus. These connections grow stronger with repetition.[24] Some neurologists say "neurons that fire together wire together" to summarize the process of learning at the neurological level. Any path that is used often becomes well worn and recognizable. Using this metaphor of a path, we can say that as traffic increases, it becomes a road, and with more traffic, a superhighway. The well worn path becomes the preferred route for any situation that requires a quick response, and the survival emotions are always on the lookout for a quick response.

Fortunately, we can also learn to stop overriding our relaxation mechanisms and start using them as they were intended. Jon Kabat Zinn has worked on teaching individuals how to relax and manage stress after their first heart attack.[25] He would be the first to agree that it is not necessary to wait for your first heart attack to learn these approaches. The meditation and relaxation exercises he teaches are based on our natural ability to relax when we are not focusing on problems and treating them as emergencies. Another teacher of meditation techniques, Joan Borysenko, describes the benefits of meditation as reported by people under pressure of real life stresses, such as terminal illness.[26]

Can we learn alternatives to the cognitive habits of depression—the automatic assumptions and beliefs associated with defeat and inferiority that develop in the crucible of the toxic shame cycle? Can we learn alternative emotional responses to these beliefs? The short answer is YES! But first we need to respect the complexity of depression.

Depression can be understood as having three components or elements: biochemical, affective, and cognitive. Let's look at them individually before we look at their interaction.

Biochemistry of Depression

Depression is associated with decreased levels of the brain chemicals serotonin and norepinephrine, which are called neuro-transmitters because they facilitate the transmission of electrical impulses from one neuron to another in the brain. In babies and other young animals, serotonin surges after nursing. When the baby is fed, he becomes happy and content. As he becomes hungry again, serotonin levels drop and he eventually becomes agitated.[27] If this state is prolonged, as in an abandonment situation, he first becomes more agitated, then listless–probably as norepinephrine levels also drop. He enters the passive state to conserve energy as we discussed above. So at an early age, abandonment or delayed feeding is biochemically associated with the affective state we later call depression. Serotonin and norepinephrine levels are also influenced in adults by diet, exercise, and rest. The proper balance can help keep neurotransmitters at optimum levels, while exhaustion due to stress, poor diet, etc. can deplete them. Unfortunately for some of us, these neurotransmitter levels are also influenced by hereditary genetic factors. Chances are good that individuals predisposed to severe depression would not have thrived in the primitive evolutionary struggles if those conditions had persisted. But as civilization and technology advanced, more depressed individuals, like those with other treatable conditions, were protected from the harsher demands of evolutionary logic so that they survived and passed on the genetic tendency for depression. Individuals with severe biologically driven depression find it difficult to think clearly and manage even simple activities of daily living without medication.

In dealing with the biochemical aspects of depression, it is useful to know that healthy diets, low in sugar and higher in Omega 3 fatty acids, can help to optimize serotonin levels. A rhythmic balance of aerobic exercise and rest can also support healthy levels of neurotransmitters. Exercise is a standard recommendation for treatment of depression.[28]

Another biochemical fact of depression is the association with increased levels of cortisol, the "stress hormone," which may be connected to the agitation of the abandoned infant, stressed with hunger, and also responsible for the disrupted sleep patterns of depressed adults. Regular feeding, healthy diet, and regular exercise help discharge cortisol and permit healthy restorative rest.[29]

Affective and Behavioral Impacts of Depression

The feelings we associate with depression are quite painful–loneliness, alienation, hopelessness, helplessness, worthlessness, agitation, and anger. We have argued that these internal emotional experiences are related to biochemical factors and evolutionary advantages. Understanding the connections can help us choose naturally corrective actions such as healthy diet, exercise, seeking comfort in supportive relationships, and getting medical help when necessary, possibly with antidepressant medications.

But it is not always so easy. Sometimes, we seek relief from the pain of depression by turning to food or alcohol or other drugs. The food may be high in sugar and give temporary relief by triggering a brief surge in serotonin levels, but will gradually undermine healthy brain chemistry as well as leading to other health problems. Alcohol or other drugs may provide brief relief by deadening the pain but ultimately prolong and deepen the depression. We feel listless and find exercise unappealing, so we remain inert but restless. Because depression is associated with shame, it leads us to withdraw from those who might nurture and comfort us. We also tend to turn the anger and agitation of depression into self-defeating, self-punishing behaviors and self-critical thoughts–reinforcing patterns of poor self-esteem in the process.

Cognitive Elements of Depression

Habits of thought are shaped by the intensity of the affective stimulus and by repetition. At a neurological level, intensity is achieved by the rapid firing of neurons (bioelectrical impulses moving through the nerve cells in the brain). This rapid firing is in itself, a kind of repetition. When the pain of depression is intense and prolonged, we teach ourselves the experience of depression and capture that learning in the way we think about ourselves and the world. Assumptions about the meaning of this painful experience are memorized. "I'm a loser." "I'm not good enough." "I hate myself." "I would be better off dead." These are thoughts typical of a depressed interpretation of life.

These thoughts or interpretations of reality become so familiar through repetition that they are no longer questioned, are assumed to be true, and become an unfortunate inner guide for behavior. "I don't deserve to be happy, so why bother trying?" "No one could care for me, so I won't bother them with my presence." "I would be better off dead, so I might as well swallow a bottle of pills." These thoughts are so thoroughly connected by our synaptic superhighways that we keep meeting them again and again in our mental travels. Through repetition we reinforce the significance of these negative beliefs, and behaviors evoked by such thoughts produce reactions in the world that seem to confirm the assumptions. Self-isolation is seen as hostile and unfriendly. Self-absorption and self-criticism are seen as unattractive. Drinking or drugging to escape the pain lead to other problems, deepening the dilemma.

Persistence of Cognitive Elements

Biochemistry can change fairly quickly, sometimes as a natural form of resiliency, sometimes through improved diet or activity, sometimes through medications that increase neurotransmitter levels. Feelings can change even more quickly in response to an intense stimulus that may compel us to act (taking action also reinforces the response) or to a change in biochemistry. But habits of thought and behavior, learned through repetition and reinforced by association with real consequences in the world, tend to be much more persistent. Long after medication has lifted the mood of a depressed person, he can continue to believe that he does not deserve to feel better. Anticipation of future failure, disappointment, or abandonment can persist even when mood is improved.

Assumptions about one's position in life, having been memorized through painful repetition, are not quickly or easily changed. These assumptions, even when the individual intellectually sees them as exaggerated or distorted, continue to stimulate affect and biochemistry that confirm the depressed world view. Medication alone, without psychotherapy to help challenge and replace the cognitive, behavioral, and affective elements of depression, will often fall short.

Once the superhighway of automatic thoughts is built to connect perceptions of external reality with internal interpretations and feelings, the network becomes a strong belief system with the feeling of truth and permanence that comes from a long history. It does not disappear quickly. And there is no way to reach into the brain and tear up the old belief system completely, although it can be challenged incrementally through repeated corrections.

Lethal Vortex of Biochemical, Affective, and Cognitive Elements of Depression

The three elements discussed above are difficult enough taken individually, but even more problematic when we realize how they tend to reinforce one another.

∞ Biochemical deficits generate feelings or affects that are painful and tend to interfere with normal resiliency.

∞ Feelings compel an inner search for solutions.

∞ The search generates or reinforces cognitive assumptions that, if misguided, lead to unhealthy habits of thinking as well as counterproductive behavior.

Shame, Anger, and Depression

∞ Repeating the depressed cognitive assumptions and behaviors generates more biochemical depression and more depressed affect, which tends to confirm the depressed assumptions.

The circular process of self-reinforcing thoughts typical of depression leaves the sufferer with the conclusion that there is no way out.

Breaking Free of Complicated Traps of Depression

Understanding the complex elements of depression and their interactions is critically important if we want effective relief from this debilitating illness. It is important to intervene in each of the elements of depression to be sure of a comprehensive approach. But where do you start?

Some people begin with psychotherapy. An initial evaluation is certainly appropriate and necessary to crafting a plan to challenge a complex depression. But if the individual is in the grip of the biochemical pall of depression and flooded with feelings of worthlessness, it may be difficult to see these depression distorted assumptions and feelings as abnormal. Exploring these feelings may provide another opportunity for reinforcing the thoughts and feelings without interrupting or challenging them effectively. As a result he may experience an increased sense of helplessness or failure when he is unable to find relief in the place where he hoped he would.

Some people begin with medication and may experience relief from the painful affect or mood fairly soon. But individual response to medication varies. The first medication tried is not always the most effective, and the trial and error process can be complicated by unpleasant side effects. Even if the mood lifts, the history of depressive thoughts and beliefs lingers. If the person has a significant layer of depressed habits of thinking and these are not challenged, the medication will not change her experience of life as completely as she hoped. She may interpret her reliance on medication as further evidence of her inadequacy. The continuing assault of depressed cognitions may undermine the benefits of the medication.

Chapter Seven

Diet and exercise would be a good place for many to start in challenging depression, but it is often difficult for someone to find the motivation or energy for these interventions when depressed. A diet or exercise partner, a trainer or support group would be helpful, but the tendency to withdraw and hide makes this effort a challenge for the depressed individual.

Similarly, social activity is also useful in interrupting depression, but shame and isolation often interfere with the social contact that is needed. Even if a person is not living alone, the shame associated with depression compels her to withdraw and the hopeless habits of thought may make her resist intervention by others. Friends and family who encourage healthy behaviors may be met with a response of, "Leave me alone–you don't understand how hard it is."

Underestimating the difficulty of breaking free of these traps can lead to unrealistic expectations of relief and more shame and anger when those expectations are disappointed. The depressed person may direct this anger toward family, friends, or therapists, or may direct the anger toward himself, fueling more extreme self-criticism and hopelessness. Although many individuals with depression can expect a good response to treatment, the complexity of chronic depression can require more persistence and strategy than is obvious at first.

A respect for the complex interaction of the biological, affective, and cognitive elements of depression requires that the depressed individual find professional help to evaluate his situation and decide on a strategic approach. Even the first steps can be difficult. It can demand courage and patience simply to find and connect with a professional the depressed person can trust. But as Richard O'Connor points out in Undoing Depression,[30] the depressed person has already demonstrated a capacity for courage and patience through the effort it takes to get through difficult days and nights. If she is able to act on recommendations for diet and exercise while participating in counseling, the strategy can be to focus on those approaches first. If she is too depressed to follow through on these recommendations, or the depression is not sufficiently relieved by these approaches, medication may be in order. If she is desperate, exhausted, or suicidal, medication or hospitalization must be recommended sooner.

Safety and stability are the first strategic goals of treatment because safety and stability are necessary for the sustained work of challenging cognitive habits, the beliefs and assumptions that have accumulated as part of the depression. By repeatedly challenging the depressive thoughts and practicing new behaviors that are inconsistent with depressive thoughts and affects, a new path associated with hope can be explored. The path, actually a mental skill, can become wider with practice, until it becomes an alternative route. For some, it can even become a superhighway to confidence and contentment.

This seems like a long haul and a lot of work for the depressed person seeking recovery. It does require persistence and repetition, but the huge task of building a superhighway can be broken down into small, easily repeatable steps and actions that can be tweaked to make them simpler. The Quieting Reflex by Charles Stroebel describes a simple six second approach to self-calming that could be easily repeated many times a day.[31] The exercise involves focusing the mind alertly while inhaling, then relaxing the shoulders and jaw with a slight smile while exhaling. By making it a point to practice this simple method hundreds of times, a familiar self-calming behavior can be established as a healthy habit. Similar approaches can be tailored to each person's preferences and experiences so that they feel natural and easy to repeat. A seemingly impossible goal can be broken down into steps so small that they no longer seem overwhelming. They can be repeated until they become automatic as recommended by Robert Maurer in One Small Step Can Change Your Life.[32]

It will also be necessary to challenge the affective habits, the long reinforced sensitivities to shame, anger, or fear that are connected to the depressed beliefs. Over time, and under the influence of depressive biochemistry or repeated traumata, it is possible to become obsessed with fear, anger, abandonment, or shame, leading to a chronic state of depression.

Chapter Seven

Fortunately, it is also possible to learn to interrupt or escape these painful affective habits through a conscious focus on images or actions that evoke patience, compassion, or an appreciation of beauty in the moment to interrupt the chronic state of emergency or despair. It is then possible to pave a new pathway in the mind connecting to a drawer in the mental filing cabinet that is filled with a collection of calming, reassuring, empowering memories and images. It usually requires guidance and a good deal of practice to do this, but it has been successfully demonstrated time and time again by ordinary but determined people who are motivated to change the way they think about their lives.

In Section Two, we will explore some of the specific strategies and techniques that can be effective in challenging the affective components of shame and anger as well as the cognitive habits that reinforce them.

Section Two

What We Can Do About Shame and Anger

Chapter Eight
Quieting Shame and Anger

For many of us, criticism can represent a threat that triggers the primal emotions of shame and anger because we learned to think of it that way at an early age. The part of our brains in charge of arousing the powerful survival emotions memorized the tone and context of criticism and assigned it the value of a dangerous event, as if we had startled a rattlesnake or stepped too close to the edge of a cliff. So we react to criticism with an intensity of emotion that makes it difficult to evaluate criticism objectively. But what if we didn't?

Occasionally you meet someone who responds to criticism without shame, anger, or fear, but with curiosity. Out of a nostalgic affection for the old 1960s Star Trek television show, let us call such a one "Spock." If memory serves me, Spock was half human and half Vulcan, an alien race that had learned to subdue the intense emotions that had brought them to the

Chapter Eight

brink of self-destruction. They had learned to operate entirely on logic. In one Star Trek episode, the crew of the Starship Enterprise finds themselves on a planet where earth culture is imitated. Spock finds it necessary to drive a mid 20th century automobile for the first time and he is not very good at it. His poor driving irritates another driver, who shouts criticism at him rudely. With an eyebrow raised, Spock seems to think, "This person expects me to be a more skillful driver than I am, and it is to my advantage, as well as in the interest of general safety, for me to become a more skillful driver. Therefore I agree with the criticism." But before he can tell the other driver he intends to accept the criticism and become a better driver, the man charges off in a huff. Dr. McCoy, having watched this exchange, rants at Spock for his lack of emotion and accuses him of being too polite. McCoy would have expressed outrage at the other driver's rudeness. Spock considers this criticism and thinks: "Dr. McCoy expects me to return rudeness for rudeness, but in my experience this does not usually improve the situation. Therefore, I respectfully disagree with Dr. McCoy and will stick with my polite and safer mode of behavior." Then Captain Kirk points out to Spock that on this planet, politeness is seen as a sign of weakness, causing people to become more aggressive toward you. Spock evaluates this new information, validates it with his own observations, and decides that on this planet it's better not to be too polite. At the next confrontation he makes a comical attempt to be rude. At each succeeding step of this encounter, he is trying to change his behavior in response to criticism that he objectively considers valid or rejecting criticism he considers invalid.

Few would choose to imitate Spock's example completely because it would seem comically robotic and unnatural, but there are times when many of us wish we had some of his detachment.

A more realistic model for emotional detachment might be the Buddhist monk introduced to us in Daniel Goleman's book, <u>Destructive Emotions</u>.³³ In the first chapter, Goleman reports on an experiment in which the monk and an argumentative professor were challenged to have a conversation about topics on which they deeply disagreed. Their physical and emotional

80

responses were monitored, their facial expressions were recorded and analyzed throughout the conversation, and they were debriefed afterwards. Despite disagreeing, the monk maintained such calm, reasonable, and compassionate attention during the dialogue, that the argumentative professor reported having difficulty maintaining oppositional feelings or behavior.

Each of us has the right to agree with criticism or disagree with it based on our own principles, our own evaluation of the situation, and the degree of respect we have for the source of the criticism. Although we may not aspire to Spock-like demeanor, most of us would agree that his model for analysis or interpretation of criticism is balanced and objective. If we hope to make the best use of criticism we would want the process of interpreting the criticism to be generally calm, balanced, and objective. Instead, for most of us, interpreting criticism is a highly subjective and emotional experience.

Each individual's response to criticism is a learned mental behavior, though strongly influenced by the primary emotions of shame and anger. We learn at an early age to interpret and respond to signs of disapproval and associate them with a sense of threat that evokes shame and anger. When these emotions are aroused, and especially when they are intense, they influence the way we interpret and understand criticism as well as how we react to it. This is true for self-criticism as well as criticism we hear from others. The main problem is that many of us have learned to react to any criticism with an arousal of shame, anger, or even fear—and often these emotional reactions are not only instantaneous, but intense. Fear, shame, and anger cause us to distort the meaning and importance of criticism.

If fear or shame dominate, we are more likely to exaggerate the truth or importance of the criticism or to make emotionally driven assumptions about the content of the criticism.

When Jeff's math teacher was preparing the class for standardized tests that would be used to evaluate the effectiveness of the school, everyone—teachers and students— felt the pressure. Jeff's math teacher, Mr. Smith, asked if there were any questions about the material he had just covered, and

Chapter Eight

Jeff raised his hand. Jeff was shy, and this, for him, was taking a chance, but his parents had encouraged him to participate more in class. Because he was shy, he had difficulty expressing his question clearly. Mr. Smith said that he didn't have time to go over it again and he would talk to Jeff after class. Jeff reacted with feelings of shame at his exposure to this perceived rebuff in front of the rest of the class. He assumed that Mr. Smith thought his question was stupid and that therefore it was stupid, and furthermore that he was stupid. He assumed that there was no point in pursuing the question, because Mr. Smith didn't really have the time and didn't want go over the question again with someone too stupid to get it the first time.

Objectively, Jeff had every right to get answers to his questions and Mr. Smith had a right to ask Jeff to wait until later if the class time was short. But when Jeff responded to what he perceived as criticism with strong feelings of shame he distorted the implications of Mr. Smith's apparent criticism. Although Jeff may seem to some readers to be over sensitive, such distortions are not at all uncommon when dealing with perceived criticism. It was an exaggeration for Jeff to conclude that Mr. Smith thought his question was stupid or that he actually was stupid, an exaggeration driven by his shame response.

When anger is the dominant emotion in reaction to criticism, there is a strong tendency to minimize the importance or truth of the criticism or to reject it altogether.

Jack saw Mrs. Jefferson coming to the delicatessen counter and quickly decided to disappear. Mrs. J was the most demanding of their regular customers, always asking a dozen questions, ordering very little, and often complaining about some detail like how much dressing was in the coleslaw. It drove Jack crazy. So he hid out in the storeroom for 10 minutes, hoping she would pass on by or one of the other servers would wait on her. No such luck. When he came out of the storeroom, she was standing right there and started right in with, "I've been waiting here for 10 minutes!" Jack rolled his eyes, waited for her to ask her questions and place her order, and thought about how he just wished she would go away.

Jack gave no thought to the "truth" of the criticism: that it was his job to wait on people at the deli counter and not to purposely avoid them. He gave no thought to the possibility that his employer might agree that he had been negligent. His irritation led him to devalue Mrs. Jefferson's complaint and justify his own behavior.

If intense emotions are aroused by the experience or expectation of criticism, and they distort our understanding of the criticism, what can we hope to do about it?

Quieting Powerful Emotions

The good news is that a number of techniques are available that help us learn to attenuate an excessive emotional response to any stimulus. Some of these have been practiced with good results for thousands of years. Some variations of these techniques have been further refined, researched, and shown to be effective in helping people with panic disorders or anger management problems. Enhancements to these techniques that have come from the practice of hypnosis, guided imagery, and neuro-linguistic programming over the last twenty years have further improved their effectiveness. There is more good news in the fact that some individuals whose anxiety, shame, or irritability is aggravated by depression can find partial relief in medication.

The not quite so good news is that most of these techniques are not as simple as taking a pill. They can be thought of as skills that require experimentation and practice before an individual can use them reliably and effectively. For an adult with longstanding emotional habits of responding to criticism with intense emotional arousal, change usually requires determination, guidance, creativity, and a lot of practice. Children, on the other hand, can learn these skills easily, just as they can learn multiple languages and music skills easily if they are given exposure to proper role models and guidance at an early age.

Chapter Eight

New Techniques

Techniques for quieting powerful emotions have been shown to be effective in treatment programs for anger management or for disabling phobias. Adults who are highly motivated can also learn these skills fairly quickly. The following examples demonstrate how these techniques can work with individuals who have problems much more severe than the typical reader. They can be even more effective in helping a motivated individual to quiet emotions of lesser intensity.

Rosemary Boerboom regularly teaches groups of men in a Minnesota state program for domestic violence intervention to control violent behavior.[34] In order to do this, they must learn to recognize the onset of angry feelings and interrupt them before they escalate into violent actions. The men Boerboom works with are highly motivated because they have been arrested for domestic violence, and they are referred to her program as an alternative to going to jail. They know that if they do not try to learn what she can teach them, they will go immediately to jail and perhaps also lose their families.

Boerboom's program is based on a twelve session model in which there is education, practice, and problem solving in group settings. Some of the men begin the program highly skeptical of the need to change or their ability to change because they believe their anger is an appropriate response to the situation and is neither their fault nor their responsibility. Most, however, eventually come to believe that they can make a change in their behavior with positive results for their family relationships. Indeed, many have made dramatic changes in their lives by learning how to quiet their anger. As they learn to practice self-calming skills, their family members feel less threatened and respond with less anger and fear of their own. The positive response of family members acts as a powerful reinforcement for the new skill.

To begin this process, Boerboom teaches a fairly simple thought interruption procedure. First the men learn to recognize the signs of anger or any negative emotion in themselves. When they notice hurt, shame, anger, or even fear, they are taught to repeat STOP STOP STOP in their minds while perhaps visualizing a flashing yellow stop sign. This creates a small break in the sequence of thoughts and feelings and gives them time to think.

Then they are taught to focus on the feeling they are having, separate it from the external triggers or events that may have precipitated it, and name it. While doing this, they must allow themselves to experience the feeling without acting on it, and to be alert to the distortions and misinterpretations of the intentions of others that might be causing them more distress. Although Boerboom does not use the word shame in her training, she does refer to "feeling unimportant, devalued, rejected, defective, worthless, powerless, unlovable, or less than human." For most of us, these terms are all associated with the affect of shame.

The third step in Boerboom's technique is to counter the shame and anger with affirmation of self-worth by stating it. "I am ok," or, "I am acceptable, adequate, worthwhile, powerful, respectable, or lovable—even if I have made a mistake and someone else is upset about it." This is often the hardest step for some individuals, because of long established habits of low self-esteem or toxic shame, which was discussed in Chapter 6. The men are supported by peer groups that help them to stick with the positive thoughts until their body language tells their peers that they really believe and accept the self-affirming statements.

Finally, having interrupted the rush of anger and defused the shame that powers it, Boerboom reminds the men that they have to choose the best behavioral option for the situation they find themselves in.

STOP (interrupt), LOOK (inside and name the feeling and recognize faulty assumptions), LISTEN (to a reaffirmation of your own worth), and CHOOSE (the best behavior for the situation) is a model that requires many repetitions in order to be effective in a highly charged emotional situation. But it does not require thirty years of training as a monk in daily meditation. This program represents one application of cognitive behavioral treatment methods, but is not the only model available.

Chapter Eight

Another source of optimism comes from the demonstrated effectiveness of treatments for phobias, techniques that were initially developed from experience with hypnosis. A phobia is a learned mental and emotional response characterized by intense and apparently irrational fear that comes to interfere with the phobic person's normal functioning. Although phobias are not necessarily associated with shame, anger, or criticism, the primary emotion of fear is similar in its intensity. The effectiveness of treatment for a phobia demonstrates how the influence of powerful basic emotions can be countered by well applied cognitive therapy. Phobias often begin with a traumatic event.

As a young man, George enjoyed rock climbing. One day while scrambling up a steep gravelly slope by himself, he pulled his head above a ledge and startled a rattlesnake. The rattlesnake rattled and startled George, who lost his grip and began sliding painfully back down about 150 gravelly feet of the slope before stopping his fall. In a few painful seconds, George's brain learned to be terrified of both snakes and heights. This incident might have been enough to install a phobic response in some people, but George was well on his way to forgetting it when he arrived for a job interview a couple of weeks later in the 8th floor office of an executive who had a vivid painting of a rattlesnake in his office. The startling picture of the snake and the view out the picture window from the 8th floor began to nag at him as he struggled to keep his composure through this important interview. The discomfort of feeling trapped in this situation was so intense that the association of snakes and heights with intense anxiety was reinforced. George began to anticipate intense anxiety whenever he had to get on an elevator and he began to expect snakes in unlikely places. Embarrassed about it, he tried to avoid such situations quietly, but he actually became more alert to the feared situations, causing him more discomfort.

Choosing to avoid a stimulus for anxiety is an active decision that tends to reinforce the association between the stimulus and the fearful response. Most of us, especially men, are ashamed of appearing fearful in public when others are not obviously afraid. We try to hide our anxiety, and the secrecy about the anxiety tends to reinforce the element of shame. George was inadvertently training himself to be consistently fearful of heights and even the thought of a snake, no matter how unlikely a snake's appearance might be. Although it is not too difficult for most of us in an urban environment to avoid contact with snakes, avoiding heights can limit our movement. George began to consciously avoid high places, anticipating that he would become anxious. And a strange thing began to happen. George found that when he was nervous about heights because he was faced with a real exposure to heights, he could not help worrying about snakes at the same time, though there was nothing real to remind him of snakes.

The brain is designed to pay special attention to anything associated with fear, danger, or pain. Once a particular memory is associated with pain, danger, fear, or shame, it can become established in your memory banks as something that easily catches your attention. Anything that reminds you of this memory may trigger a surge of anxiety or shame, and focusing on the memory may bring a stronger surge as more details trigger more anticipatory fear. In this way we automatically practice staying alert to those things we consider dangerous, and of course it is good to be alert to danger—up to a point. The problem is that we can become over-sensitized not only to dangerous realities, but also to our own scary thoughts, and this can get out of hand.

George began to realize that his nervousness about heights and his inappropriately fearful thoughts about snakes were far out of proportion to the actual danger, but he couldn't help himself. The fear seemed to paralyze him and leave him feeling shaky even when he knew he was safe. This embarrassed him because of his past comfort with heights and risky situations, and the embarrassment added shame to anxiety, making him even more distressed. George decided to get help. He consulted two therapists and asked them on the phone about their approaches before setting an appointment.

The first therapist described a classical desensitization protocol for dealing with phobias. In this treatment, George

Chapter Eight

would first be taught about the nature of anxiety, including the physical and emotional and mental response to fear. He would be taught to recognize the sensations of fear or anxiety and label them when he experienced them, simply by saying to himself, "My heart is pounding because I am feeling fear or anxiety." He would then be taught a self-calming technique that would include breathing and relaxing exercises along with a method for realistically assessing the danger. He would be coached to practice the self-calming exercise until he became very familiar with it and proficient at it. Then, in a safe environment, he would be asked to think of something that usually made him anxious and notice the signs of increasing anxiety. Before the anxiety became too intense, he would be coached to practice the self-calming exercise until the anxiety receded. With several repetitions of this, George would gain confidence in his ability to relieve the anxiety rather than having it escalate painfully. When he was skilled at dealing with the anxiety provoking thoughts, George would be helped to face real life situations that might trigger the anxiety surges, always with appropriate plans for real safety such as moving away from the edge of a precipice. With practice, George would establish a new mental and emotional response pattern that would free him from the exaggerated panic of the phobia but leave him with a healthy respect for dangerous situations.

This therapist told him about a book he could read and even try some of the exercises on his own, noting that many people found they could get better results with some direct therapeutic support and guidance through the procedures.

The second therapist George spoke to agreed that the classic procedure was usually quite effective, but told him that some people were able to benefit from a quicker, shorter treatment if their phobia was simple and associated with a specific traumatic event. The shorter approach might be worth a try with the understanding that the classic approach could still be used if the new approach was not sufficient. Both approaches were based on an understanding of how the mind processes fear and how phobias are learned.

Quieting Shame and Anger

George decided to try the shorter approach and made an appointment with the second therapist. First the therapist took a history to establish that the problem did seem to come from a fairly recent and simple trauma for which George had a clear memory. The therapist then asked George to describe some situations in which he felt completely safe and comfortable, and "anchored" those memories and feelings by patting him on the shoulder and saying, "That's good." The physical and verbal stimuli of the therapist patting him on the shoulder and saying "that's good" were designed to be associated in George's mind with the feelings of safety and comfort evoked by George's positive memories. The therapist could then help George to maintain feelings of comfort and safety throughout the rest of the exercise. Finally, he asked George to vividly imagine himself in a sort of private movie theater to replay the memory of the original trauma from beginning to end several times, with some variations while the therapist occasionally patted him on the shoulder and said, "that's good." After about ten minutes, George was asked if he still felt terrified when he thought about the accident. George was surprised to hear himself say no. He was asked to think about other situations involving heights, and he reported no abnormal anxiety. Six months later, George's phobia had not returned and he had successfully dealt with plenty of situations involving heights and even a visit to the snake house at the zoo.

The second technique described above is similar to approaches used by practitioners of neuro-linguistic programming (NLP), a set of treatment approaches that evolved from a study of effective hypnotherapy. NLP practitioners are trained to observe their clients' responses carefully and to suggest a variety of techniques tailored to the individual's reactions. Practitioners of Eye Movement Desensitization and Reprocessing (EMDR) report similar results in relatively short treatments.[35] The sooner a person seeks such treatment after a traumatic incident, the more successful it is likely to be, though some sufferers of post-traumatic stress have found relief many years after the traumatic incident.

Another model, one based on ancient traditions and skills for quieting the emotions comes from practitioners of meditation and yoga who for thousands of years have been able to demonstrate an ability to quiet the mind and body to a remarkable degree. These skills were considered exotic and inaccessible to skeptical westerners until fairly recently, when researchers like Herbert Benson, author of The Relaxation Response,[36] confirmed their effectiveness and demonstrated that even very simple practices of self-calming through regular meditation brought physical and emotional benefits.

Using yoga or meditation as a technique for calming powerful emotions requires repetition for learning. Regular and diligent practice focusing on something positive and peaceful helps to exercise the areas of the brain where contentment, calm, and joy are experienced. In order to maintain this focus, the practitioner learns to avoid the distractions of discomfort, impatience, or "the destructive emotions" (so labeled by Buddhist teachers because they "destroy" compassion, harmony, and enlightenment). Gently refocusing from fear to compassion, from anger to compassion, from desire, shame, hunger, or pain, to compassion—thousands of times over years of practice—the meditator learns how to remain calm in the face of threat or provocation. It doesn't matter whether the threat comes from outside or from one's own imagination. Beginning meditators do report some benefits fairly soon after starting their practice, but default reactions to long memorized threats do not change quickly. All of the methods described above require some level of determination, commitment to practice, and repetition in order to be effective, but some approaches can reduce the time and amount of practice and repetition required.

Neurofeedback, a new technology that is receiving increased attention for its positive results, allows individuals to train their brains using a computer program that gives them visual feedback on their brain activity. Electrodes placed on the scalp read the types of brain waves ranging from the slowest, (Delta waves) associated with deep sleep, to the fastest (high-end Beta waves) that are consistent with emergency problem solving activity. Quite often, people with problems having to do with affect regulation or difficulty in focusing their attention are either over-aroused or under-aroused in terms of brain wave activity in the areas of the brain needed for optimal functioning. There is now striking evidence that people can use computer driven feedback programs to inhibit chronically over-aroused brain wave activity and stimulate under-aroused activity to find the optimal balance so that they are not trying to operate their brains with one foot on the accelerator and the other on the brake. Individuals can use the visual and auditory feedback, presented in the form of a video game, to practice achieving the optimal balance for them. Researchers in neurofeedback report improved concentration states and improved regulation of emotions. It has been used to help those with attention deficit disorders to learn to focus and those with anxiety disorders or anger management problems to improve their affect regulation, both of which reduce frustration and secondary shame. Cognitive therapy allied with such techniques can help individuals achieve better regulation of toxic shame with resulting improvement in self-esteem.[37]

Learning to Quiet Shame and Anger

The process of intentional change begins with a decision to change. For most of us, the need for change in our emotional response to criticism is a personal determination. We alone decide whether our experience of shame and anger are excessive and detrimental to our happiness or effectiveness. Some of us will get feedback from those close to us indicating a problem with shame or anger.

Jim was the CEO of a small corporation. He had a tendency to be quite impatient and irritable. Though he was vaguely aware of this, he did not consider it a problem until he sought the services of an executive coach to improve his leadership skills. The coach urged him to participate in a "360 degree evaluation process" in which all of the people with whom Jim interacted provided the coach with their reactions to and assessment of Jim's leadership qualities. They all understood that the information would be handled confidentially and only shared with Jim in an appropriate manner in order to facilitate improved communications and work relations. The coach would take responsibility for talking to Jim about the results. When the results came in, Jim discovered that many of the people around him reported feeling intimidated by his tendency to scowl or bark his disapproval, often over a very minor disagreement. Although his subordinates had learned that this was "just his style," they were still reluctant to approach him when he looked irritable, and they were especially reluctant to deliver bad news. This limited the information flow in the organization, as well as their own creative risk-taking, and therefore made Jim an inhibiting factor in the office operations. Jim was shocked to receive this information and reacted with his accustomed impatience and irritability, inwardly criticizing others for their misinterpretation of his behavior or their oversensitivity. He was responding to the criticism he perceived in this feedback with anger, rejecting the criticism automatically. Then, at the end of one hectic Friday, a young and promising staff member delivered a less than positive report. Jim immediately snapped at her and watched the color drain from her face. In that instant he saw the impact of his anger and realized that the feedback he had received was true. He was angry too much of the time and it was influencing his effectiveness. Once he accepted this, he realized he needed to change and became highly motivated to learn to tame his anger. Because he was proactive, Jim immediately read one of the recommended books on anger management. The book outlined a number of exercises. The exercises focused on interrupting anger as soon as he became aware of it, and there were a number of suggestions for how to do this. He could see a stop sign flashing in front of his face and say to himself, "Stop! Stop! Stop!" while breathing deeply and slowly. He could ask himself, "Do I really need to be angry to solve this problem?" He could stretch and smile to change the physiology associated with anger and break the tension mounting in his body as well as his mind. He could begin to remind himself of times when a calm listening approach worked better. After reading about these techniques and practicing some of them, Jim returned to the coach for more guidance.

Quieting Shame and Anger

Habitual anger can become such a common experience that it is possible for someone not even to notice his own feelings. Jim had become so accustomed to being angry that he did not notice it until others pointed it out to him. The same can be true of feelings of shame. Affect theorists believe that shyness and self-consciousness are ways in which we react automatically with shame to social exposure, just as Jim reacted automatically with anger to many situations. Some people are shy or self-conscious so much of the time they do not even realize it could be otherwise.

Susan was embarrassed twenty times a day. She blushed at some of the most inoffensive things, and some of her friends teased her about it, which made her blush even more. As the middle child of an otherwise boisterous group of five siblings, she had always considered herself "the dumb one," though her grades in school clearly demonstrated otherwise. She had learned as a child that asserting herself in her family risked making her the object of jokes, so she tried never to stick out. This habit was so familiar to her that she assumed no one would see her as especially capable or impressive. Nonetheless, she was encouraged to accept a promotion that would require giving presentations to small and medium-sized groups. She soon found herself so sensitive when she was the center of attention that her embarrassment quickly escalated to acute anxiety. A friend suggested she see a counselor to help her overcome this limitation so that she could advance her career. Susan was sure that there was nothing that could be done about it. She thought it was just the way she was and always had been. With encouragement from her friend however, she agreed to meet with a counselor who specialized in this kind of problem.

The counselor first asked background questions to make sure that she had not had traumatic experiences in life that might underlie her shame response. It seemed that she had always been shy and this embarrassment reaction had grown over the years as she contrasted herself unfavorably with her extraverted siblings. After an explanation of the shame response and the change protocol that would be used, and after brief examples of how the imagination and physical changes in facial expression, breathing, and posture could affect emotion, Susan was less skeptical and willing to give it a try. The goal would be to learn to quiet the rapid and intense shame response to a number of insignificant everyday triggers. She could then use that skill to consciously quiet shame in other situations as she determined best. Susan wanted reassurance that she would not be "shameless," a person with no self-restraint, or someone others would find egotistical. The counselor explained that the shame response was normal and would always be there for her as a signal to keep her from transgressing her own moral standards or exposing herself to social risk, but it would not have to be so painful and extreme that it paralyzed and limited her. She was told that she would always be the one who would decide how much quieting of the shame response she wanted. Susan was satisfied with these answers and committed herself to a course of 10 to 12 sessions to learn the emotional skills necessary to begin to quiet her overactive shame.

Both Jim and Susan were introduced in their separate counseling experiences to a variety of exercises and approaches similar to the ones George had learned about in his efforts to deal with anxiety. Some were cognitive therapy strategies by which they were taught to identify recurring thoughts that would arouse shame or anger. After identifying them, they would learn to question or challenge these thoughts methodically whenever they became aware of them.

Jim learned to question the universal sense of urgency that he discovered underlying his angry thoughts. He found that he tended to assume everything had to be done right now, even though this was often unrealistic or even unnecessary. This tendency generated frustration over the things he could not control and led to a simmering impatience that fueled his temper. Jim was also taught that he could shift his mood by changing his posture, his breathing, and his facial expression. Because emotions are physical responses, changing the physiology helps to change the emotion. Shifting from anger to a more neutral or joyful emotional state allows more freedom in thinking. Jim learned that when he was angry or impatient he was more likely to make assumptions or believe thoughts that were associated in his mind with urgency and anger. When he was not angry, he was freer to entertain other assumptions.

When Jim was able to shift his mood away from anger, he discovered that it was easier to challenge or question the thought patterns associated with anger, because he was no longer riveted on the focus of his frustration. Jim also learned that he could soften his mood and shake off frustration by breathing deeply, stretching, and smiling while he thought about a quiet vacation spot, one associated with relaxation. With practice, Jim found that he could cut his exaggerated sense of urgency and frustration significantly, and he was pleasantly surprised when his wife and youngest son were the first to notice his new mood. People at the office, however, were slower to trust the change. For them, Jim had become a trigger for fear, anger, or shame. Though they observed a difference, they would not comment on it until Jim admitted that he been working on stress and frustration management and asked directly for feedback. Then his colleagues admitted to noticing a change and were willing to approach him about problems with less fear of negative reaction. When they discovered Jim was able to listen to problems and even to some criticism without blowing up, they were impressed. Jim discovered that problems were solved more creatively when he could listen more calmly.

Susan found the cognitive therapy approach more difficult. She could not easily identify any thoughts associated with her embarrassment. To her it seemed just a sudden intense feeling that came over her in social situations. Many thoughts and memories associated with her embarrassment seemed to come later, but when she was feeling embarrassed it was hard to stop and notice what she had been thinking. The counselor pointed out that Susan had experienced shame or embarrassment in family situations when she was very young. She had learned embarrassment so well that it had become an automatic and intense internal response to the stimulus of being the center of attention. In order to change this Susan would have to learn and practice new emotional responses to these situations, and this could be done through structured or guided use of her imagination.

Chapter Eight

Susan was asked if she could remember any time when she was having so much fun that she forgot to be embarrassed. She remembered a relay race in which she had been required to participate in grade school. She was the last member of her relay team and her team was ahead, but not by much. Even though she was the center of attention with teammates cheering for her as well as others cheering for her opponents, she was so caught up in running and winning that she did not feel embarrassed during the race. After the race was won and she was being congratulated, her embarrassment returned. The counselor asked Susan to focus on the memory of the moment when she was in the race and feeling excited instead of embarrassed, and to memorize that moment and hold onto it as a mental emotional resource. The counselor explained that keeping the sense of focus and excitement of the race in mind could help interfere with the usual shame response and help her to learn a new emotional reaction to the stimulus of being the center of attention in everyday situations. Susan tried this in the counseling session, but was having difficulty keeping the excitement of the race in mind. The counselor added another step. First he asked Susan to think about the race, and when Susan remembered the race experience with all the physical intensity of running as fast as she could, she was given a spongy ball to hold in her hand and squeeze. While she was squeezing the ball, she was encouraged to think about an embarrassing event with part of her mind's eye while still squeezing the ball and remembering the race with another part of her mind. Finally she was asked to follow a pointer with her eyes as the counselor moved it back and forth in front of her face while Susan continued to keep the race and the other events in mind. This complicated but structured mental task helped Susan to blend the two different emotional reactions in her mind and when she was asked to think about the embarrassing situation again, she was surprised to notice that the intensity of the embarrassment was much less. After this procedure was repeated three more times, Susan reported that she could think about the problem situation with very little embarrassment. She was amazed at the dramatic change.

Quieting Shame and Anger

Susan was then coached on a handful of "shame interrupting" behaviors that she could experiment with and practice. Because the typical posture and facial expression of shame includes bowing the head, averting the eyes, and frowning slightly, Susan was encouraged to stand in an exaggerated upright posture as if a string was attached to the top of her head, stretching her spine. At the same time she was encouraged to look up and out rather than down, and to smile slightly and calmly. When she was able to get herself to do all these things, she reported a decrease in her usual feeling of self-consciousness. Adopting a posture of pride can interfere with the shame response. Because shame is the posture of defeat, soldiers are trained to stand tall and proud, even when the drill sergeant is shouting insults at them. This helps them resist the impulse to surrender in stressful situations.

Susan was also encouraged to focus intensely on external visual and auditory stimuli. The conscious mind can only focus on a limited number of stimuli at any one time. The external visual focus, even on ordinary objects like the fabric of her skirt or common sounds like the slight ringing in her ears, would distract her from an automatic tendency to monitor internal sensations of shame and self-deprecating internal analysis.

The old habits were deeply ingrained and Susan had to practice these techniques often to make a difference. But the fact that she could actually notice a difference was encouragement enough for her to continue. The more she practiced, the more her confidence grew, and the painful habits of self-consciousness gradually began to fade.

George, Jim, and Susan each had their own reasons for wanting to change. Each had a different emotional response that needed adjustment, and each was willing to do what was necessary once they learned what was possible.

Many people afflicted with painful emotional responses do not seek help and therefore do not learn what is possible to achieve with commitment and practice. Instead, they continue to endure unnecessary anxiety, anger, or shame that complicate their lives and compromise their happiness. Some will turn to drugs, food, or other destructive behaviors to find relief, ultimately generating more shame and hopelessness.

In order to make a decision to change an emotional response pattern that may seem to be a part of your personality, it may be useful to ask yourself some questions to help rate the extent to which these patterns are causing problems. A few standard questions can be found on the next page to help you make this assessment for yourself.

This part of the book is designed to let you know about the possibility and potential benefits of such change, and some of the approaches that are available. The motivation to do the necessary work comes from a combination of your own assessment of the need for change, your desire for change, and your belief in the possibility of change.

Quieting Shame and Anger

SELF TEST FOR EXCESSIVE EMOTIONAL RESPONSE

Ask yourself questions 1-8 below. If the answer to question 8 is yes, questions 9 and 10 may help you begin to build motivation for change and clarify goals by giving you a positive example to model.

1. Do I often experience anger, anxiety, fear, or embarrassment?

2. Have friends or family members commented on my anger, anxiety, or shyness?

3. Have I avoided situations that I associate with anger, anxiety, or embarrassment?

4. Does such avoidance represent a sacrifice on my part?

5. Have I been awake at night reviewing a situation in which I was angry, anxious, or ashamed?

6. Do strong emotions make it difficult for me to communicate effectively with others?

7. How often do I resort to behaviors to control anger, anxiety, or shame that may not be good for me or those close to me?

8. If I could reduce the intensity and frequency of these emotional reactions, would I be better off?

9. Who do I know who has better emotional management skills than I do?

10. How would my life be better if I could react the way they do?

Chapter Nine
The Criticism Connection

Now that we have discussed how to recognize the powerful automatic emotional responses to criticism and understand that shame and anger can be quieted by a variety of approaches, we are ready to apply this understanding to the difficulties we have in receiving criticism.

Many individuals discover their own reasons for quieting negative responses to criticism and quickly figure out methods to tame feelings of shame and anger.

Pam had the responsibility of explaining her government agency's regulatory policies to groups of business people and other citizens affected by the policies. Frequently, they were not shy about criticizing the programs she was presenting and in which she had a personal investment, having worked to create them. She soon discovered that if she became defensive and argued with the critics, the animosity increased. Over time,

The Criticism Connection

she trained herself to listen patiently to this feedback, to consider the audience's point of view, to mine it for potentially helpful suggestions, and to ignore the rancor. In the process, she found that her respectful listening won her allies among the audiences for her presentations and helped her communicate ideas more effectively.

For thousands of years, and in every generation of humankind, confident individuals have exhibited a response to criticism that minimizes shame and anger and gives them the best chance of learning from the critical feedback of others. A very few seem to be able to react patiently even when attacked with malicious and unjustified scorn. They appear to have learned that their own internal responses are potentially more damaging than the words of the critic. By calming their internal responses, they maintain their balance in the situation and can judge for themselves the truth or value of the criticism.

A recent visit to the Wushu School of Kung Fu outside of Beijing afforded me an opportunity to talk with the young students following a demonstration of their skills. I was impressed by their gentleness and poise. Although I do not know the details of what goes into Kung Fu training, some of their discussion suggested that a large part of their training involves learning to focus their attention and energy (their *chi*) and not to waste it in the expression of shame or anger. Similarly, young Tibetan monks learn a style of debate that is characterized by mutual respect and affection. All disagreement is prefaced by a symbolic reminder of this respect and affection when the monks twirl their prayer beads above the head of their debating partner to chase away the "mistaken" ideas. They learn through daily debate practice how to accept criticism from their peers without attaching shame and anger.

No matter how confident we may be, however, almost all of us have our areas of vulnerability. We struggle with resentment and feelings of hurt or defeat in response to criticism without realizing that we can learn to listen without the shame response and sometimes to make criticism work to our advantage.

Chapter Nine

Values Clarification

When someone is criticizing me he is contrasting my behavior, or something about me, with a standard, an expectation, or a value that he thinks should apply to me. If I agree with the value he holds, I can accept the criticism and learn from it. If I disagree, I can reject the criticism, or rethink my values, or ask him to rethink his. He can use all kinds of persuasion and social pressure to influence me, and I can use all the powers at my disposal to influence him, but the final decision about values, and therefore the decision to accept or reject criticism, is in the control of each individual who faces criticism. Successful response to criticism requires that each of us accept the responsibility for choosing our values and matching our behavior to our values.

When we are young children, it usually does not feel like we have much of a choice. We are dependent upon these powerful people, parents and teachers, who hold most of the cards. We have to accept values and criticism from them or endure consequences we do not think we can tolerate.

By the time we are adults, however, we are expected to take full responsibility for our choices and the values on which they are based. We are increasingly challenged to defend our values by critics who have different values. At some point along the way from childhood to maturity, the decision about how I should act changed from being their decision to being my decision. For many of us, it is not quite clear when and how that happened and how, exactly, we are supposed to make these decisions for ourselves. We may stumble along in a fog of indecision with varying degrees of shame and anger, accumulating assumptions about values along the way without learning how to evaluate these guidelines and confirm them for ourselves. We may accept the values of our peer groups or families in order to avoid the threat of criticism or ostracism, without thinking clearly about whether or not we really agree. Or we may reject the values of family or peer group in an attempt at self-definition that can also be contaminated by shame and anger over anticipated criticism.

The Criticism Connection

In order to accept full responsibility for our choices, we must take time to think clearly about the standards, values, and internal guidelines on which these choices are based. Parents and teachers often try to teach the values they want their children to adopt. But it is much more challenging to teach children how to make their own value choices and confirm them clearly for themselves. The pressures of maintaining order in the family and school social systems limit the amount of choice parents and teachers are willing to allow young people. Many of the values are imposed as rules with little debate allowed for fear of the chaos that might ensue. As a result, many reach the age of personal responsibility with a good deal of confusion about the internal values and standards that guide their own behavioral choices, creating a need for a process that has come to be known as "values clarification." Values clarification provides a framework for clearly thinking through what you believe is most important, and memorizing it so that it provides a ready guide for behavioral choices in real time.

A good example of this process is the "personal mission statement" described by Stephen Covey in The 7 Habits of Highly Effective People.[38] Covey refers to the personal mission statement as an "internal compass" to which we can refer for guidance once it is carefully constructed and calibrated. He suggests several exercises for establishing one's own personal mission statement and describes general principles that are useful to keep in mind. But he is careful to emphasize that each individual is responsible for choosing, clarifying, and memorizing the values and standards that go into her own personal mission statement, the points on her own internal compass. Choosing, clarifying, and affirming one's own values is empowering. It provides a solid foundation from which to respond to criticism from others who may have different or ill-defined values.

The process of developing an internal compass is not something that can be completed on a given afternoon, although it may be possible to make a pretty good start by following Covey's suggestions and drawing upon past life experience. The internal compass is best conceived as a work in progress that is refined and improved across an entire lifetime. At each moment in time, we must choose as well as we can, based on the values we then understand, but we can continue to refine and clarify the values that make up our internal compass. In this lifelong endeavor, criticism from others can be an aid as well as a challenge. Not only does a clear internal compass give us a solid base from which to evaluate criticism, but critical feedback provides information we can use to further clarify our values, either changing them or confirming them more clearly through our analysis of the criticism. This is only possible, however, if our analysis is relatively free of the shame and anger that so often clouds our judgment.

Limiting Habits of Thought

Shame and anger are not the only things that cloud our perceptions and interfere with clear and effective decisions in real time. Some assumptions and habits of thought are misleading or completely false, but are so familiar that they are taken as truth and guide our behavior in important ways. Such "cognitive distortions" or beliefs based on "automatic thoughts" are the subject matter of cognitive therapy.

Cognitive therapy focuses on the thoughts and assumptions that may be false or distorted and therefore causing problems with effective decision making or with self-esteem. These may be statements about myself, such as, "I'm so lazy, I'll never succeed." Or, "No one could ever love me." Or, "I just don't have a head for that kind of work." They may be assumptions about others, such as, "He is such a tough guy, nothing could hurt his feelings." Or, "She is too popular to hang around with me." Or, "He really must hate me because he disagrees with everything I do." Frequently, automatic thoughts draw from a disappointing interpretation of past experience and generalize it into the future, making us feel defeated before we even try. Cognitive therapists help their clients to recognize the limiting operation of automatic thoughts and unquestioned assumptions, to challenge them, and eventually, to replace them with thought habits more supportive of success and self-esteem. The impact can be most dramatic when an individual realizes he is making

The Criticism Connection

the same kind of mistaken assumptions over and over again and is able to succeed in challenging those assumptions in a few instances with positive results.

Jamie just knew the math homework would take hours and he would never be done in time to watch the show he wanted to watch. It was always hard, and he was always so frustrated that it took forever to settle down and get started. Then he would be so frustrated that he couldn't concentrate. This conviction had been established over years in response to his parents' belief that homework should be easy for him because he was so bright. When he first began to confront more difficult assignments his frustration led to self-criticism that made it even more difficult for him to concentrate. He tried to avoid this frustration by putting off his homework with a dozen distractions until it really did seem that homework assignments took hours. His parents' frustration at his procrastination added to the tensions.

When his parents hired a tutor to help him, Jaime was suspicious that this was just someone intended to force him to study longer. The tutor surprised him, however, by telling him that he would only have to work for five minutes on the first assignment. Indeed, he would only be allowed to work for five minutes on the first lesson. Then he would be done—lesson over for that day. The only goal was to see how many math problems he could finish in five minutes so they would have a way to measure progress in the future. The math problems didn't even have to be all correct. The goal was just to finish as many as he could in five minutes. After plenty of reassurance that this was not a trick, Jaime agreed and got down to work. After five minutes, he was surprised to discover that he had finished six problems and that five of them were correct. The entire assignment was only 25 problems, but the tutor insisted that they stick to the agreement to stop for the day.

In the next tutoring session, the tutor gave Jaime a choice to work for seven minutes or to stick to five. Jaime chose seven minutes and completed 10 problems. Although the tutor insisted on sticking to the time limit, Jaime finished the other 15 problems before school the next day in about 12 minutes. He was beginning to challenge his old assumptions that doing the math homework would take hours. A few successes was all it took for him to revise his old belief and begin to be confident that he could concentrate effectively for short periods of time. Gradually, he grew confident in his ability to concentrate for longer and longer periods of time.

Cognitive therapy with adults typically begins with an understanding that the way we think about our situation influences how we feel about it. Identifying the most limiting or damaging distortions is a first step to challenging and replacing them. A motivated individual can learn to challenge a habit of thought repeatedly that keeps him from succeeding ("I could never run a marathon.") and replace it with a more optimistic but realistic thought ("I can run a half mile to start and gradually build my endurance."). When this procedure is diligently and persistently applied, changes in thinking take place. Research with obsessive compulsive patients who are tortured by automatic thoughts and behavioral habits indicates that measurable changes in brain activity patterns can be achieved through persistent application of cognitive therapy practices.[39]

Sometimes getting the distorted assumptions and counterproductive emotions out of the way will be all that is required to open the door to positive new habits. Freed of the interference from shame or anger or self-limiting automatic thoughts, some individuals quickly find a way to develop new skills and new confidence. Some readers will have already begun to apply the information about shame and anger, challenging cognitive distortions to their own habits of responding to criticism, and finding ways out of the traps of criticism that have troubled them in the past.

Because we learn most efficiently by imitation, however, it can be helpful to provide a template or a model for a new habit to replace the old habits. Learning a new response to perceived or overt criticism is like learning any new and complex skill. It is best to learn the fundamental steps first in a

The Criticism Connection

low pressure situation, then to string the fundamental skills together into a sequential combination. After that, it is necessary to practice until both the fundamental skills and the complex string become familiar and comfortable. We do not attempt to learn to ice skate under the emotional pressure of competitive performance. We separate the practice of basic skills from the anxiety of performance by learning in a safe and supportive environment first.

A Neuro-Linguistic Model for a New Response to Criticism

In the last thirty years, some individuals who were both curious and creative decided it would be great if they could learn how naturally confident people respond to criticism and teach others how to do the same. These individuals invented Neuro-Linguistic Programming (NLP), a set of techniques utilizing the knowledge of the way people store, retrieve, and manipulate memories to make decisions in everyday life. They studied naturally confident people to create models for a variety of emotional skills that others could learn. NLP offers particularly effective approaches for reducing the emotional distortion attached to criticism. This can be important for those who have an especially strong and immediate emotional reaction to criticism. As we discussed earlier, experiencing criticism through a lens of shame makes it more likely that you will assume the truth of the criticism, while experiencing criticism through a lens of anger tends to make you discount or ignore it. Reducing the emotional impact of the criticism is therefore helpful in evaluating criticism objectively.

NLP accomplishes this partly by using the relatively safe environment of one's own imagination (like the athlete rehearsing mentally before performance), along with structured steps and repetitive practice, usually under the guidance of a professional experienced in helping people learn mental and emotional skills.

One of the most important goals in the NLP approaches that I use in my practice is to achieve an affective shift away from shame and anger to one of interest or even excitement. Evoking the emotion of curiosity about what we can learn from criticism helps us to reduce the influence of shame and anger and focus on the values involved in the criticism. For this reason, I like to call the exercise described below "A Curious Response to Criticism."[40]

Curiosity is important because it offers an intellectually interesting and emotionally engaging alternative to the defensive response we usually have to criticism. At the moment I am criticized, I can respond by being curious about what I will discover when I compare my values to those of the critic as I analyze the criticism. I can be curious about how this will impact my own decision about the validity of the criticism and about how this decision will inform my future actions.

This exercise is a variation of a protocol I learned 15 years ago in a training class for NLP[41] and have been using with clients ever since. Because there are several steps with detailed instructions, many people find they can learn it more quickly and easily if they are led through the steps by a professional or someone familiar with the exercise. Others find it quite useful in written form because it allows them to practice the exercise at home. The instructions for the "Curious Response to Criticism" exercise are complex, so I will present it in distinct steps with instructions for each step presented in **bold** with explanations following in regular text. Examples of applications are included.

The Criticism Connection

Learning a "Curious Response to Criticism"

I. Imagine that you are in a special movie theater designed to help you learn to respond well to criticism.

Most people experience a normal form of dissociation (a separation from your own physical experience) at the movies. They forget all about the other patrons, the spilled candy and soda, and the marginally comfortable seating, and become absorbed in the movie experience—allowing their emotions to be influenced predominantly by the sights and sounds on the screen. Imagining a movie is a subtle invitation to a safe and familiar form of dissociation.

II. In the movie theater of your imagination, you're going to see yourself learning a new way to understand criticism. As soon as you're comfortable, let the lights go down and see yourself on the screen being criticized by someone–not the harshest criticism you've ever had, just a minor criticism.

III. As soon as the criticism is heard, imagine that you go to a small movie within the movie to interpret the criticism.

This complex instruction is referred to as double dissociation and tends to engage the creative imagination so thoroughly that little mental attention is left for shame and anger reactions.

IV. In this second imaginary theater there are four screens,
like a window with four panes. Take a moment to visualize
a grid of four screens clearly.

The Criticism Connection

V. On Screens One and Two at the top, you will see the criticism situation from the critic's point of view–what he thinks you did and what he thinks you should have done, according to his values. If either of these is not clear to you from the critic's words, it will be important to get clarification from the critic. If the critic is unwilling or unable to give clarification, consider the possibility that this is careless criticism or emotional bullying that you should dismiss.

Screen One	Screen Two
What the critic thinks you did	**What the critic thinks you should have done**

VI. On Screens Three and Four, at the bottom, you will see the situation from your point of view–what you think you did and what you think you should have done based on your own values. If your own views of your behavior or your expectations are unclear or unrealistic, you will find that you can not make a clear picture for comparison. This is important to recognize and correct. Unrealistic expectations of yourself can be as destructive as others' unrealistic values.

Screen One What the critic thinks you did	Screen Two What the critic thinks you should have done
Screen Three **What you think you did**	**Screen Four** **What you think you should have done**

The Criticism Connection

In looking at your actions on Screen Three it is important to be very honest with yourself. In the privacy of your own imaginary movie theater, you can safely ask, "Did I do that? Did I do what the critic says I did?" It is always tempting to avoid shame by distorting your view of your behavior so that it is consistent with your values. The private movie theater of the imagination provides an opportunity for a balanced and honest view. If it is based on a clear and honest perception, your conclusions will be most valuable and useful to you.

Deciding what to display on Screen Four is difficult if you are unsure of your values on the issues being criticized. Many of us have not thought through our own behavioral expectations so that they are clear and specific. This sometimes happens when a person is accustomed to accepting other people's values from an early age and doesn't stop to question whether he agrees with these values or not. If this is the case, you will need to spend some time thinking through what you believe is really important for you on the subject under criticism. As we have discussed above, values clarification is an important exercise in itself, and identifying situations in which our values are not clear can prompt us to refine our internal guidelines.

VII. **When the scenes on all four screens are clear, you are going to compare all of these pictures and decide how much of the criticism you agree with.**

Option 1 - You can decide you agree with the critic's observations and values and accept the criticism. In this case you can decide to behave differently in the future and may even want to tell the critic that you agree with his perceptions and values and plan to act differently in the future.

Bill's remembered criticism featured a time when his boss criticized him for repeated tardiness. On Screen One, he saw himself coming in late and on Screen Two he saw himself coming in on time, which represented the observations and expectations of his boss. Screen Three, representing his own perceptions of his habitual tardiness, and Screen Four, representing his belief that people really do have a responsibility to show up for work on time, matched those of his boss. Basically, he agreed that he should be on time, but often wasn't. When he stated his agreement and his commitment to work harder to be on time, his boss was satisfied that he understood the criticism, and when Bill followed through on his commitment, his boss noticed and approved.

Option 2—You can decide you disagree with the critic's observations of you even though you share his values. This is not simply a matter of defending yourself against the sting of criticism. If it is clear to you that the critic thinks you did something you did not do, it may be helpful for both of you to try to correct that misperception. It is not always possible, however, to convince a critic that his observation was mistaken because sometimes his perception is based on misinformation from another source, which you may or may not be able to correct. Sometimes, you must be content to know the difference in your own mind when you discern that attempting to correct the critic's perceptions is only triggering more criticism.

Francine remembered a time when her sister criticized her for borrowing her favorite sweater without asking. On Screen One, Francine saw her sister's perception of her doing just that. On Screen Two, Francine saw her sister's expectation of her asking and being given permission. On Screen Three, Francine saw her own memory that she had not taken the sweater at all, with or without permission. On Screen Four, she saw her own expectation that she should ask for permission before borrowing something, a value she shared with her sister. In Francine's example, she agreed with her sister's expectations and values, but disagreed with her sister's assumption that she had taken the sweater. She rejected the criticism and the problem was only resolved when their mother told them she herself had taken the sweater to the cleaners.

Option 3—You can decide that you agree with the critic's values and want to revise values you have held previously. This provides an opportunity to refine your internal compass by rethinking your future expectations of your own behavior.

David came under regular criticism from his wife for watching too many violent shows on TV, but he defended his right to watch whatever he preferred. Screens One and Two, represented his wife's view of his behavior (watching violent shows) and her values (not watching violent shows). Screen Three, representing his behavior (watching violent shows— which he agreed that he did) and Screen Four representing his values (watching whatever he liked) were initially consistent with one another and different from his wife's view. As time passed, however, David began to question the value of the shows he often watched and came to believe that he added to his own stress as well as supporting violence on TV by watching them. Although he automatically tuned in to the same shows for some time, he began to agree more and more with his wife's view and was motivated to try to choose other activities with less violence and stress.

Option 4—You can decide that you agree with the critic's observations of you, but disagree with his values. After reexamining your values, you decide you want to reaffirm them.

As a young graduate student, Joe embraced liberal politics and disdained the accumulation of wealth, taking a stubborn pride in driving old cars and wearing mostly jeans and sweatshirts. Later in life, when his eco-tourism business flourished and generated significant profits, he and his wife Judy maintained their commitment to living simply, donating significant amounts to charity while saving some money for college tuition for their two children. When the kids were grown, Joe's father encouraged him to invest aggressively for retirement, but Joe and Judy continued to give much of their income to charity. Joe's father criticized him for being financially irresponsible and putting his family's security in jeopardy. Joe understood his father's concerns and respected his opinion. After discussion with Judy and careful reflection,

Chapter Nine

however, they agreed to stick with the values they had practiced together since they met rather than to begin to accumulate wealth at this stage of their life. Screens One and Two, representing Joe's father's observations and values were clear. Screens Three and Four, representing Joe's self-observation and values also remained clear and consistent, even after thoughtful review. Joe maintained and was comfortable with values different from his father's.

You are the only one who can choose the values and expectations you want to live by. Listening to criticism can help you refine your values or tune up your behavior, but the critic cannot make decisions for you about your values.

VIII. Now, watch yourself up on the screen absorb the information and make a decision about the criticism. Now watch yourself on the screen repeat this process with at least two other examples of criticism. Notice any signs of growing confidence and clarity in the posture and facial expression of yourself up on the screen.

This entire process is a skill which you can learn best by applying it to simple examples of criticism first. As you master the skill and gain confidence in it, you will find that it can be applied to more complex and more significant examples of criticism where it will be necessary to clarify the critic's complex expectations and your own values. The facility of the human mind for this kind of analysis is astounding, but there is a chance of becoming confused when trying to tackle complex examples before the fundamentals have been learned.

IX. When you believe that you have mastered this method of evaluating criticism for your own benefit, imagine that you come down off the screen and merge with the you sitting in the theater so that you now have that learning inside. Take just a moment to let that sink in before the lights come up and you leave the imaginary theater to go on with your life.

X. Finally, take a deep breath in the real world and rehearse three or four examples of possible future criticism,

The Criticism Connection

applying the curious response to further consolidate the learning.

One of the most important elements in the exercise described above is the affective shift from the emotion of shame or anger to the emotion of curiosity and readiness to learn from an experience of criticism. Some individuals with whom I've worked have had great difficulty shaking off the automatic shame or anger response to criticism. Some of them have found it helpful to imagine themselves in learning situations they found more evocative of curiosity than a movie theater. A few have imagined that they were staring through a binocular microscope to watch the criticism exercise play out. For them, this imagery elicited a sense of more intense concentration. Others found it more curious to imagine they were in a hot air balloon looking down on the learning experience from above. One gentleman imagined that he was seated comfortably on the bottom of a swimming pool and could see the criticism exercise contained in large air bubbles that rose slowly to the surface. One young woman mentally borrowed some of the scenery from a recently released Harry Potter movie as the setting for her learning. It seems to me that approaches that feel creative and imaginative to specific individuals are more successful in evoking an attitude of curiosity that neutralizes the unwanted shame or anger.

Another possible asset or tool in shaking off the automatic shame or anger response is the memory of strong positive feelings associated with some past experience or relationship. For example, one young woman was only able to relax with this exercise when she remembered the warm, unconditional love she felt from her maternal grandmother. Only while imagining sitting with her grandmother, basking in the warmth of her smile, was she able to view the criticism examples without slipping into shame and anxiety.

As with any new skill, repetition and practice is necessary for the skill to become smooth and automatic. Subtle changes can be made to the process to suit the individual. Some clients have reported that they notice small physiological changes as they practice. They may experience a tendency to take a deep breath and exhale slowly as they quickly analyze the criticism, for example, or cock their head to one side or raise an eyebrow to evoke curiosity. These little refinements are very idiosyncratic and often happen without the individual noticing at all.

Learning a new response to criticism does not erase the old response. If you have always reached your travel destination by a certain route, it becomes so familiar that it is almost automatic. If you discover a new route, you may have to concentrate on the new directions at first to keep you from taking the old route automatically. If the new route is an improvement, you now have a choice. But the old route does not disappear. With practice, the new route becomes automatic, but the old route is not completely forgotten for many years, if ever.

So it is with mental emotional habits, which are like pathways built of multiple synaptic connections in the brain. Discovering a choice comes first. Exercising the new choice— practicing choosing the new response—strengthens the new response. Eventually it becomes the default response.

A Review of the Steps

I. **Imagine that you are in a special movie theater designed to help you learn to respond well to criticism.**
II. **In the movie theater of your imagination, you're going to see yourself learning a new way to understand criticism. As soon as you're comfortable, let the lights go down and see yourself on the screen being criticized by someone—not the harshest criticism you've ever had, just a minor criticism.**
III. **As soon as the criticism is heard, imagine that you go to a small movie within the movie to interpret the criticism.**
IV. **In this second imaginary theater there are four screens, like a window with four panes. Take a moment to visualize a grid of four screens clearly.**

The Criticism Connection

V. On Screens One and Two at the top, you will see the criticism situation from the critic's point of view—what he thinks you did and what he thinks you should have done, according to his values.

VI. On Screens Three and Four, at the bottom, you will see the situation from your point of view—what you think you did and what you think you should have done based on your own values.

VII. When the scenes on all four screens are clear, you are going to compare all of these pictures and decide how much of the criticism you agree with.

    a. Option 1—You can decide you agree with the critic's observations and values and accept the criticism.

    b. Option 2—You can decide you disagree with the critic's observations of you, even though you share his values.

    c. Option 3—You can decide that you agree with the critic's perceptions and values and want to revise values you have held previously.

    d. Option 4—You can decide that you agree with the critic's observations of you, but disagree with his values.

VIII. Now, watch yourself up on the screen absorb the information and make a decision about the criticism. Now watch yourself on the screen repeat this process with at least two other examples of criticism. Notice any signs of growing confidence and clarity in the posture and facial expression of yourself up on the screen.

IX. When you believe that you have mastered this method of evaluating criticism for your own benefit, imagine that you come down off the screen and merge with the you sitting in the theater so that you now have that learning inside. Take just a moment to let that sink in before the lights come up and you leave the imaginary theater to go on with your life.

X. Finally, take a deep breath in the real world and rehearse three or four examples of possible future criticism, applying the curious response to further consolidate the learning.

Chapter Ten
How to Deliver Criticism
Without Shaming

Although most of this book has been directed at understanding the emotional impact of receiving criticism and learning how to moderate our responses, the fact is that we all deliver criticism as well. This chapter focuses on how we can give criticism as effectively as possible, without shaming the person we are criticizing. There are many good reasons for giving criticism and some that are not so good.

Good Reasons for Delivering Criticism

There are many relationships in life in which it is appropriate to criticize, to give another person feedback about his behavior and ask him to change it.

How to Deliver Criticism Without Shaming

∞ Parents need to guide their children, to teach them how to behave in society, how to accomplish things, and how to stay safe in dangerous situations. Although teaching by example is always important, parents cannot teach effectively by example alone. When safety is involved, parents cannot wait for the child to notice what the parent is doing, but must give pointed direction and corrective feedback to ensure that the child pays attention to the lesson. A parent cannot stand patiently at the curb, for example, while a child runs into the street, unaware of the danger of oncoming traffic. We will discuss the dynamics of shame in parent-child criticism in Chapter 11.

∞ Teachers who are charged with training children and others to meet certain standards of knowledge or skill must give students critical feedback. To the extent that we expect our teachers to help shape socially acceptable behavior as well as imparting knowledge and instilling technical and academic skills, they will need to criticize in many of the same ways that parents do.

∞ Supervisors and other organizational leaders who are responsible for the work output of a group will have to correct subordinates when their work is not up to a defined standard, and may also have to intervene if the subordinates are not cooperative with one another in creating a productive work environment.

∞ In our day to day interactions with friends and family, we sometimes need to let them know when their behavior has hurt us and ask them to respect our feelings and perhaps change their behavior. This involves another kind of critical feedback that is vitally important in maintaining healthy and honest interpersonal relationships.

∞ There may also be times when we find the behavior of a stranger unacceptable, or even dangerous, according to our understanding of societal norms. We may legitimately try to intervene. This kind of criticism almost always runs a high risk of evoking a negative reaction, however.

Chapter Ten

∞ Finally, we may be directly asked for critical input by another person and want to respond constructively. In this situation it is important to remember that criticism can be both positive and negative. When my wife asks me how I like her new dress, I try to frame my answer very carefully.

In each of these situations, it helps to be clear about the purpose of the criticism in the context of the relationship you have with the person you are about to criticize.

Less Noble Reasons for Giving Criticism

But, of course, we don't always stop to think about the nature of our relationship or the purpose of criticism in the heat of the moment. Criticism is often given simply because we are irritated, anxious, angry, scared, hurt, or some combination of these emotions. We want the other person to back off, apologize, change, or do it the right way (our way). In such cases, criticism has a good chance to go awry, triggering shame and anger in the recipient rather than respect and understanding.

And then there are times when we make casual judgments about others without any expectation that they will change and with the full knowledge that they will disagree. On these occasions, we just cannot seem to keep our opinions to ourselves. The result is that the other person rightly feels criticized and responds with hurt or anger.

Venting Anger as Criticism

Sometimes, when we are angry, whether the cause of the anger is or is not clear, we vent the anger in behavior that sounds and feels like criticism. People around us see what looks like critical behavior and hear what sounds like criticism, and they jump to the conclusion that we think they have done something wrong. Children are particularly vulnerable to this kind of event.

When Geoff stomps into the house irritated by problems at work and a tiring commute, he doesn't have to say anything for the kids to become nervous. It is enough that he is acting like he is in a bad mood. If he trips on a toy and grumbles loudly about the mess in the house, the family members are correct to conclude that he is criticizing, but the intensity of the criticism is disproportionate to the mess, and this is confusing. Giving criticism when you're angry about something else carries this risk—and it is a common occurrence.

Venting anger may be an effective and appropriate method for some people to reduce the intensity of their frustration so that they can shift into problem solving mode. If you want someone else to listen to your venting, however, it is important to be sure they do not mistake it for criticism and that they have the time and emotional detachment to be able to listen without becoming upset. If they have not agreed to listen, they may react to your venting as unfair and exaggerated criticism or even emotional abuse. The simplest way to determine if they are willing, is to ask. "I've had a terrible day and I just need to blow off some steam. It would help me if you could just listen. Is that ok?" If you are talking to someone who cares for you, a positive reply is almost guaranteed.

Giving Criticism to Raise Your Status

In elementary and middle school, children often react to their own shame or low self-esteem by teasing, criticizing, or blaming others. Sometimes this has the effect of shifting the focus of blame from one child to another. Sometimes it makes him a temporary celebrity as he gets attention for making someone else the focus of scorn or the butt of the joke. In either case, the goal is to make himself feel good, or at least a little better than he was feeling, even if the blaming or teasing results in someone else feeling worse. Whether it occurs among children or adults, this amounts to emotional bullying. In addition to the immoral aspects of making one person feel better at the expense of another, there is the risk of retribution. Some of the school violence that has made headlines in recent years has been attributable, at least in part, to revenge taken by victims of cruel teasing or emotional bullying or ostracism. In adult life, thoughtless blaming or teasing can result in office feuds or power struggles that undermine productivity and personal effectiveness. In home situations it can ruin a marriage or seriously damage the self-esteem of children.

Controlling Behavior to Calm Anxiety

Many people are beset with anxious feelings that they try to calm by keeping their environment under strict control. They tend to have rigid behavioral standards and preferences that lead them to constantly correct those about them for even the smallest of deviations. These "corrections" are frequently not viewed as criticisms by the anxious person who gives them, but rather as obviously needed adjustments to something that seems "wrong" and therefore anxiety provoking. For those who are corrected, however, particularly family members and co-workers who are corrected again and again, this behavior feels like criticism and evokes full blown shame and anger reactions that can ultimately destroy the closest of relationships if not brought under control.

Careless Criticism

Of course, all of us have occasionally hurt the feelings of friends and family with casual, unnecessary negative judgments. We live busy lives, and the time pressures we find ourselves under make it seem as if we live in a state of emergency. Under such pressure, we react with quick judgments that can be thoughtless and sometimes hurtful. Increased awareness of the risks of such criticism can be established as an inner warning system if you want to learn to avoid hurtful, critical behavior. We can, if we truly want to, learn to pause long enough to think carefully before saying things like:

∞ You're wearing that!?

∞ Well, it's fine if you like orange, I guess.

∞ That's not the way we do it here.

∞ What's wrong with you?

∞ Boy, that was dumb.

Expanding upon these uses of criticism and their negative impact on both the person criticizing and the person criticized is beyond the scope of this book. Assuming that you do not want to use criticism for these purposes, there is still a chance that you will accidentally vent your anger at times and in ways that others perceive as critical. You may also give in to the temptation to tease or blame others when you yourself are feeling attacked or vulnerable. Most of us experience occasional periods of insecurity when we just want to have our own way and tell people what to do. And, of course, all of us get careless. When this happens, recognize the misstep, apologize to the person you may have hurt, forgive yourself, and try again.

If the goal of your criticism really is to influence another's behavior with positive or mutually beneficial intent, it is important to deemphasize shame and anger as much as possible. Because criticism is so often given for the wrong reasons, or in the wrong way or at the wrong time, and because we learn our emotional responses to criticism when we are young and vulnerable to all but the most sensitive delivery of criticism, it is understandable why many people are suspicious of or sensitive to criticism.

Constructive Criticism

The problem for the constructive critic is that he or she runs a high risk of being confused with all of the destructive critics encountered by the person being criticized. When constructive criticism fails because it triggers shame and anger, time is wasted, opportunities for positive change may be lost, and relationships can be damaged.

A quick internet search on giving criticism will yield a variety of articles by human resource specialists and others on constructive criticism. Constructive criticism is generally defined as criticism that:

- ∞ Provides feedback that enhances job results or family cooperation
- ∞ Leads to ongoing personal and professional development
- ∞ Reduces stress and creates psychological security
- ∞ Helps improve interpersonal relationships

Chapter Ten

∞ Helps develop an improved organizational or family climate

Most of these articles agree that giving criticism is a delicate matter and that the critic should strive to be clear, brief, calm, thoughtful, and to deliver the criticism in private rather than in public. Some encourage sensitivity or a balance between positive comments and negative comments to reduce the chance of a painful reaction. Others suggest that "sugar coating" criticism with compliments may be confusing to the recipient, like disguising anger with humor.

The point of criticism is that the critic thinks there is room for improvement for one of the reasons listed in the bullets above. This point should be made clear, along with the reasons the critic believes improvement is needed, how specific improvement is possible, and how important it is to the critic, organization, or family.

Sarah is a highly competent and sensitive nurse, who is very thorough in her treatment notes on patients. When the utilization review manager in the hospital explained that the nursing notes may be beautifully written, but that the hospital will not receive its accreditation unless they consistently adhere to a specific format, the reason for the criticism was clear and Sarah responded immediately.

When the critic is applying his own personal criteria and expecting others to take it seriously, he must be prepared to explain and defend those criteria if he wants the criticism to be accepted. The boss who orders things to be done his way "because I say so," will get half-hearted or partial compliance at best.

Another common problem is that clarity often suffers when the critic is too verbose. The meaning and the importance of the criticism is lost in excessive detail and the listener loses focus and motivation. Over-detailed criticism becomes punishment by a thousand boring cuts, and the recipient defends herself by forgetting half of what is said. The critic who can be brief, getting to the point clearly, will still have an audience when he is finished and is more likely to have a positive response.

Balancing positive and negative comments can have value in delivering criticism. To my mind, the best example of this is illustrated in The One Minute Manager[42] by Blanchard and Spencer. The authors stress that a reprimand is best structured as a brief expression of disappointment in a subordinate's performance followed by a positive statement of belief that he can do better. They believe that this positive ending to an instance of criticism has the best chance of motivating the subordinate to try harder to meet the expectations of his boss. They also stress that the expectations must be realistic, based on an accurate assessment of the subordinate's ability and experience and supported by providing the subordinate with training and opportunity to take more and more responsibility.

Criticism of Creative Work

Most of us have had the experience of realizing that criticism we delivered resulted in a negative response we did not intend.

Vin was an art teacher who tried to be clear with his students in the illustration class about the intention behind his critique of their work. He wanted them to be prepared for the feedback they would get from future employers and the standards those employers would apply. When he received inadequate submissions for one assignment, he displayed them in the front of the class and began critiquing them frankly, one by one, in a manner that he thought was humorous enough to soften the impact. When he turned from the art to face the class, he was stunned to discover more than one student in tears and others either comforting fellow students or looking stricken themselves.

Vin was initially chagrinned and a bit defensive, but he later regrouped and took a second look at his style of presenting criticism. He was greatly helped by an article by Liz Lerman, a choreographer, on the system she had developed for structuring peer criticism for a piece of creative work.[43]   He resolved to incorporate it into his teaching methods.

Lerman outlines several steps for offering criticism specifically oriented to artists who may want feedback on their work. Most of these steps can be modified to fit other relationships and critical situations as well, but they are particularly well suited to giving feedback on any endeavor that involves personal creativity.

Step One: Affirmation

Beginning with praise indicates a respect for the courage it takes to present creative work in which the artist has invested time and effort as well as personal exposure. She suggests using positive comments about the work such as "surprising," "unique," "poignant," "interesting," or "compelling."

Step Two: Artist as Questioner

Lerman's process suggests that the artist be encouraged to ask for specific, rather than general, criticism. This can be facilitated by a group leader or a mentor to help the artist frame and ask questions to solicit specific feedback.

Step Three: Responders Ask Questions

Lerman suggests that critics, whom she calls "responders," frame their initial responses gently in the form of neutral questions to further clarify the purpose of the criticism. A questions such as, "What were you trying to accomplish with this piece?" prepares the way for specific feedback on whether the viewer's experience of the work meets the artist's expectations.

Step Four: Opinion Time

Lerman suggests that when the criticism has been framed as described above, it is still appropriate to further clarify the artist's request for feedback by saying, "I have an opinion on a direction you could go. Do you want to hear it?" This allows the artist to control the pace of the criticism by acknowledging that they may not be ready to take in this feedback.

How to Deliver Criticism Without Shaming

When my wife was editing the text of this book, there were many times when she had useful ideas about improvements. She usually wanted to voice them when they were fresh in her mind, but I was not always in a state of mind that would allow me to pay attention and accept them positively. I found that if I said so, and asked her to make a note to herself so we could discuss it later, the process of revision went forward more smoothly.

Step Five: Subject Matter Discussion

The next step allows for a discussion about the responders' thoughts and reflections in reaction to the work being discussed. This has to be managed to prevent it from becoming tangential or over detailed so that it is confusing rather than focused and helpful.

Step Six: Working on the Work

The final step is for artists who want to and are able to immediately revise their work in response to the criticism process. An actor may try a part of a scene again to see if the revised performance works better in the view of the critic, a poet may change a word or a line to improve her work, but it is less likely that a sculptor or film maker will be able to make immediate revisions during the response session.

Lerman's process leans heavily on positive comments to take the sting out of criticism and the structuring of criticism so that the artist asks for specific feedback and controls the pace of the feedback to avoid being overwhelmed by the potentially shaming impact of criticism.

The importance of sensitivity and attention to structure in giving criticism can apply to many situations in which the "creative endeavor" may not strictly be considered artistic, but for which sensitivity to the creative effort is important nonetheless. These may include your opinions of a neighbor's redecorated living room, a child's book report, or a worker's memorandum, to mention only a few. When time constraints seem to preclude sensitive treatment of these matters, consider the amount of time that would be required to repair a relationship damaged by hasty criticism.

Chapter Ten

Assertiveness as a Model for Effective Criticism

Another approach to giving criticism is based on principles of assertive communication. Assertive, in this case, does not mean aggressive, hostile, or negative. In the literature on assertiveness most writers emphasize that the goal is effective self-expression. I like to define assertiveness as the art of asking for what you want in a manner that makes it easiest for the other person to hear and respond positively.

If the goal of your criticism is to change the behavior of the person you are criticizing, the assertive option is to come right out and ask for the change directly. If I'm criticizing you, I am asking you to do something differently, to make a change now, or to try to make a change in the future. Unless I am asking you to make a change, my criticism is only an insult, an expression of anger, or a statement of disapproval with no expectation of change. Unfortunately, the specifically desired change is often left vague in criticism. Statements like "You're too sensitive," implies some need for change, but what and why is unclear. "This doesn't work," or "You're acting like a child," leave the person being criticized with the responsibility of filling in the blanks regarding what would work or what acting like an adult would be like in this critic's view in this specific instance. These statements only indicate "I think what you are doing is bad or wrong." It does not describe the other behavior "I think would be better."

An assertive approach to criticism places less emphasis on what the other person has done wrong and more emphasis on how they can do better—better, at least, in the view of the critic.

Skillful assertiveness involves:

1. Stating your reason for giving the criticism, including your feelings and the purpose or goal of the criticism;
2. Describing the desired behavior in contrast to the observed behavior as specifically and realistically as possible;
3. Asking for the desired behavior; and
4. Remembering to say thank you.

How to Deliver Criticism Without Shaming

Let's explore each of these steps.

1. Stating Your Feelings

Anger has a valid place in the expression of criticism. It tells the listener that you feel strongly about what you are saying and you want them to pay attention. A little anger is an effective attention getter. Too much anger usually has the effect of driving people away, arousing their defenses, or generating a shame response. So it is important to know your own feelings in the process of delivering criticism. Are you angry? Impatient? Confused? Hurt? Worried? All of the above? Acting automatically without knowing what you are feeling can send confusing signals, make confusing demands, get confused results, or worse.

Basic emotions are directly connected with physical behavior such as facial expression and body language. We all learn to read and pay attention to these affects before we learn the sophisticated verbal language for feelings. Therefore, it is pretty hard to hide our feelings from one another, and when we try, we usually succeed only partially. The result is that we send mixed or confused nonverbal signals about what we are feeling. If a child observes facial expressions and voice tones of irritation and we deny feeling angry, he is confused and feels helpless to know how to react. If the child is quite sensitive to anger, he may react with so much defensiveness that it is hard for him to listen to the details of what you are trying to say. And it is not just children who react this way.

It can help to acknowledge or state your feelings for a number of reasons. If you think of criticism as a <u>request</u> for respect and change, rather than a <u>demand</u> for change, you may have a better response from the recipient. Assertiveness principles suggest that asking for what you want can bring a better response than demanding it. In addition, the other person is more motivated to listen to your request if they understand how important it is to you. Understanding your own feelings and stating them or expressing them in a reasonable way can help motivate someone to listen to your criticism.

When Jane comes home from work and finds that the children have left a mess in the kitchen, she could yell at them and tell them to clean up their mess immediately. Sometimes that might be the degree of anger that would be most effective. But if she notices that they have begun to tune out her yelling, she might try a different tack.

As a directly assertive approach, Jane might take a deep breath, find the appropriate child, get his attention, make eye contact, and—cutting right to the request—say, "Will you clean up the sink while I ask your sister to take out the trash?" If this does not get a positive response and is no more successful after a couple of repetitions, she might say, "Look, I am really tired from working and fighting the traffic to get home, and I was looking forward to relaxing a little bit. I am disappointed and ticked off that I have to clean up the mess that you left before I can even start dinner. It would help me a lot if you would come and clean up the kitchen without complaining, or help me with dinner or both. I know nobody likes to clean the kitchen, but it would make things a lot easier for me. Will you do that?"

Assertiveness (as an alternative approach to criticism) works because it is less likely to evoke the shame or anger response, though it is still possible for the listener to react with shame or anger that they evoke for themselves in response to an assertive request. A critical statement without an assertive request might sound something like this, "Why do you always have to leave such a mess? Haven't I told you a thousand times not to leave a mess in the kitchen? Do you think I should have to clean up your mess after working all day to put food on the table?" The problem with all of these expressions of anger and criticism are that they do not allow for a helpful response. Even if the children answer the rhetorical questions and accept the criticism, there is nothing they can do about it but feel attacked and ashamed and, sooner or later, angry. By offering a solution and assertively asking for it, the critic (Jane in this case) creates an opportunity for things to improve. By letting them know how she feels about it, she increases the importance of their response. And if they do respond positively, she can reinforce the solution by thanking them, even if she thinks they should have done better in the first place.

2. Describing the Desired Behavior

In order to make an assertive request or give criticism effectively, it is important to know what you expect of the other person. It is also important that those expectations be realistic and specific. If your criticism or request is based on vague or unrealistic expectations, you are, in effect, expecting the other person to guess what you want or need. And their guess may be wrong. As much as you might want to shift the responsibility to them, you are taking a chance if you leave the interpretation of your needs up to them. You may be disappointed in the result, and the other person will also be frustrated. One way to test whether your criticism or assertive request is specific and realistic is to see if you can imagine the other person actually doing what you want. Can you see, in your mind's eye, a short movie of the behavior you are expecting? Do you know from past experience that they have done this thing before? If you can imagine them doing it, but you do not know if they have ever done it before, you may be asking them to learn something new, making this a more complicated request. Is it realistic to expect that they could do it in the time available and with the resources at hand? Unless your expectations are realistic and specific, your criticism may evoke shame and resentment, but not compliance, and your request is likely to be ignored or misunderstood.

3. Asking for What You Want

You have acquired the person's attention and let them know this subject is important to you. You have described the desired behavior and how it differs from the behavior you find objectionable. When you let them know why this is important to you, you can be sure that the other person will accept your criticism. Right? Not quite!

The key to assertiveness—after being clear about what you want, is asking. Let's say I am getting ready to leave my parking space when you pull up and block me in. I could say, "Where did you learn to drive, idiot?" Or I could say, "Can't you see that I'm getting ready to leave?" Or I could ask, "Will you please pull up a few feet so that I can get out?"

Even when the need is clear and simple, it helps to ask—clearly and politely—and if need be, persistently. Why? Because a question clearly requires an answer and a request is a question. If I ask, "Do you understand my criticism?" The other person may answer yes, but nothing happens. But if I ask, "Will you do what I am asking?" and the other person says yes, they are volunteering to comply. Because they have agreed, voluntarily, to your request, they are more likely to follow through than if they are ordered to do something.

When I tell you to do something and you submit to my order, it makes you feel like a subordinate or inferior, and usually triggers shame, unless you are in a social organization like the U.S. Armed Forces, where it is well understood that there is honor in following an order from a superior.

If, on the other hand, I ask you to do something for me, I am subtly acknowledging my need and your ability. This is flattering and respectful compared to giving an order, and the other person may grant your request simply because it makes him feel good to be able to do something for someone else—or because he enjoys the respect that comes with being asked.

The more important the request is to me and the easier it is for you to grant, the more likely it is that you will say yes.

Finally, if my criticism or complaint is complex, requiring a lot of effort on your part to change, I will do well to break it down into smaller requests that are easier for you to agree to.

4. Getting to Thank You

In the classic book about winning negotiations, Getting to Yes,[44] the authors point out the importance of framing a win-win situation in order to gain the agreement of the other party. They recommend resorting to threats only as a last resort and only when you are absolutely sure you are willing to follow

How to Deliver Criticism Without Shaming

through. When you choose to criticize by asking assertively for a change, the most natural quid pro quo to offer in return for their "yes" is your gratitude—your thanks. Along with the gratitude goes the implication that you will be willing to reciprocate, to consider their request for change when the time comes.

There are many refinements to skillful assertiveness that I will not attempt to repeat here. Books on assertiveness such as The <u>Assertiveness Workbook</u>[45] or <u>The Complete Idiot's Guide to Assertiveness</u>[46] go into much more detail on how to develop and refine assertive communication skills. The important point to remember for our purposes is that most criticism can be expressed in the form of an assertive request. And if your request is realistic, specific, and skillfully delivered, you may be successful in getting all the way to "thank you," and both parties will benefit from the interaction.

Assertive asking and getting to thank you builds positive relationships rather than eroding them. Each time someone asks for help or asks for a change, gains agreement, and says thank you, there is a positive exchange between two people. If you think of a give and take relationship as a small economy, asking and getting represent one trade. The more trades in the economy the more resilient and vibrant it is. So when you get some "no" responses to your assertive requests, it is less disappointing because you have had plenty of yes responses. This can only happen if both parties are willing to ask frequently, and the balance of trade in this small economy is fairly even.

The assertive individual who asks and receives from many other individuals also becomes more confident that he will be able to get what he needs, even if he experiences consistent "no" responses from one particular person. Based on a history of positive responses, he experiences his social world as generally supportive, full of yeses.

Contrast this with the experience of someone who never asks because they don't want to burden anyone else or depend on anyone else. This person may have the same needs and may be able to meet many of them himself, but he does not enjoy a growing confidence in the giving and getting of support from others. More than likely, he assumes that his requests will be denied, so he experiences a private disappointment built into this assumption. When this person does have needs, and he anticipates a rejection, shame and anger over the anticipated disappointment may provoke the hostile criticism with which most of us are familiar.

Many people in the United States value independence and self-sufficiency. Perhaps it is the heritage of our colonial and pioneer history that makes us proud of our ability to do for ourselves. But the reality is that most of us depend on a great many other people every day for things that we take for granted, without asking and without saying thank you. This value of self-sufficiency, even if it is an illusion, tends to make it shameful to ask for things and therefore inhibits assertiveness that helps build interdependence and healthy communities.

Therefore learning to ask assertively for the change or the help you want rather than criticizing when you don't automatically get it becomes a more complicated business. We must overcome the shame of asking and practice assertiveness until the consistent rewards of assertiveness reinforce this behavior. Like learning a language, music skills, or self-calming, learning assertiveness can be a snap for a child when she is raised in a family where assertive asking, rather than reflex criticism, is practiced consistently. Parents wishing to cultivate this practice can make a game out of it, reframing complaints and criticisms into assertive requests.

You can try it for yourself without anyone else knowing. Each time you catch yourself ready to voice a complaint or criticism, stop and think, "What do I want to happen?" If you don't know what you want to happen, what is the chance that the other person will guess it and respond positively? If you do know, you can ask yourself, "Is there a way I can ask for that straightforwardly without the sting of criticism? How much do I need to tell the other person about why it is important to me? And how can I express it simply, clearly, and maybe repeatedly so that I can get what I want and get to thank you?"

Whether using an assertiveness model, a one minute manager model, the Liz Lerman process, or some other

How to Deliver Criticism Without Shaming

approach, certain common guidelines are always worth remembering when giving criticism.

Timing and Structuring the Criticism

Nobody likes to be surprised with criticism. It can help the other person to listen better if they know what to expect. Sometimes the situation is structured so that the purpose of an interaction is understood to involve criticism. When a teacher meets with a student to review a paper or test, or when a supervisor meets with an employee for a performance evaluation, there is often a structure that is intended to prepare both of them for the task of sharing critical information. A performance evaluation may be based on specifically defined job definitions and performance objectives. The student's understanding of the learning objectives is often not as clear. Although learning objectives are sometimes clearly defined in college, graduate school, and job training programs, it is rare that high school or middle school teachers will expect their students to listen to a definition of goals for their own learning. In either case, however, it can help to review the overall purpose of the interaction.

Time and Place

Much criticism can wait for an appropriate time and place. Supervisors should try to make a private appointment with a subordinate rather than delivering criticism spontaneously in front of co-workers. Parents and teachers should try to talk seriously to children privately about sensitive matters rather than risk shaming them in front of their social competitors, whether these are siblings or peers. This can be difficult, especially when the youngster involved tries to avoid a private confrontation. But the effort to be sensitive to shame issues is better than casually or thoughtlessly delivering important criticism in front of others. When criticism is delivered in front of others, the recipient is distracted by the discomfort of the situation and angered by the shame. Therefore the criticism is unlikely to be heard, understood, or accepted.

Chapter Ten

Getting Their Attention

Asking for attention and securing it before beginning with the criticism is also helpful. If Sally launches into a complaint, or even an assertive request, when Jack is watching the Red Sox win or lose the final game of the American League Championship, she will not only not have his full attention, but the irritation of having his game interrupted will be added to the shame and anger reaction to hearing criticism. The results are not likely to be satisfactory. If she waits for a better moment and says, "There is something important I need to talk to you about as soon as possible. When is a good time?" she is more likely to get his attention. After she has his attention, she can also notice whether or not he continues to focus while she describes her concern and her request for change. If she notices certain non-verbal cues that his mind is wandering, or if he interrupts her to change the subject or defend his behavior, it will be important to pause and regroup to be sure she has his attention.

Bearing in mind the potentially shame inducing impact of criticism and carefully structuring its delivery according to the steps outlined above can help tremendously in avoiding misunderstanding and the shame and anger laced reactions that are highly corrosive to relationships.

Chapter Eleven
Implications for Parenting

Children come into the world equipped with feelings—powerful emotions—for which they have no words. In the course of their infancy and childhood they will learn how to manage these emotions for better or for worse, and of course, their first teachers are their parents and siblings. The more you understand about these emotions and how to manage them, the better you will cope with the frustrations and challenges of family life and the more you can teach your children about how to cope with disappointment, hurt, rejection, and criticism.

Without awareness of these emotions and a clear plan, we have a strong tendency to repeat the same parenting behaviors we experienced as children. Children absorb complex behaviors by imitation, and it is easy to catch a five year old practicing her parenting skills on her doll, teddy bear, or younger brother.

Chapter Eleven

These memorized skills, however poorly understood, emerge when we find ourselves in the role of parent because they were memorized and associated with a specific time in life. Sometimes we are shocked to discover that we are using the same parenting approaches, even the same words, our parents used with us even though we disapprove of some of those approaches in retrospect and remember the words as punitive or shaming.

Most new parents simply don't know that they must think through and practice alternative behaviors if they wish to raise their children in a different manner than their parents raised them. This chapter will help you identify those areas on which you may need to focus attention and spend time learning alternative behaviors.

Shame and Normal Socialization

Shame and forgiveness or reconciliation play an important and necessary role in the socialization process of children in families. Every child will inevitably try dangerous or unacceptable behaviors in the course of exploring new experiences. She may run into the street chasing a butterfly or bite a playmate who tries to take a toy she is playing with. The necessary restraint or scolding that the parent applies in response will trigger some shame and distress. If the scolding is followed by an offer of affection after the child shows acceptance or understanding, the shame is released and the child is motivated to learn a more acceptable behavior.

In the daily vicissitudes of family life there are opportunities to balance censure with reconciliation, scolding with reassuring affection. A "time out" procedure replicates the rhythm of shame and reconciliation. If this is done consistently in response to the child's behavior, the child will learn that some behaviors bring scolding and a taste of shame, but the chance for reconciliation is never lost.

If, however, the scolding is too harsh, the shaming lasts too long, and reconciliation with approval or affection are not offered soon enough or at all, there is a good chance that the shamed child will find his emotional release in the surge of aggression that follows shame. He will cease to seek reconciliation and turn to defiance.

Self-Awareness in Parents

Most parents are quick to get over the disappointments and frustrations of interactions with their children, especially when the children are young. But these aren't the only frustrations in a parent's life. Pressures at work, a long daily commute, and money worries are only some of the stressors that exist in the life of almost every family. Young children are quick to read the emotional body language of the most important people in their environment, but they are not experienced enough to know whether the signs of anger or disappointment in their parents are caused by events at work or at home. They react automatically as if the emotions expressed by their parents are caused by or directed at them. And it is not unusual for an accumulation of anger that may have started elsewhere (at the office or on the beltway) to be triggered into expression by frustrations at home, so it seems to the child that he caused the outburst. Until they are old enough to know otherwise, children are likely to assume that if you are angry, you are angry at them, and they react with anxiety or shame, triggered by the overwhelming importance of an angry parent. Their shame will then be followed by some of their own aggression or anger because, as we have discussed, that is the way we are wired.

The parent who is aware of his own anger and the impact it is likely to have on his children can choose to practice self-calming, or he can choose to attenuate the expression of anger so that children are not confused by excessive exposure to this dangerous emotion that feels so overwhelming to them. Denial or even suppression of the anger is not as effective as self-calming, however. Children are acutely attuned to the body language of powerful emotions in their parents, so when Jimmy notices that Dad looks and sounds upset, but Dad denies it, Jimmy is confused—suspecting something is wrong that he can't understand. This leads to anxiety and perhaps some sense of foreboding or failure that may translate into shame. So when Dad says, "I was in a bad mood earlier, but I took a walk and now I feel better," and Jimmy reads the body language and sees that this is true, the anxiety, shame, and potential anger Jimmy may feel can quickly evaporate.

A parent who is careless in the expression of anger or criticism may unintentionally subject his children to a barrage of minor traumata that lead to excessive early shame and anxiety, sensitizing the child to these emotions and influencing the development of patterns of emotional processing and expression. Learning self-calming strategies after you have grown up with a different model for dealing with frustration is not easy. A variety of creative approaches can be applied, but all require practice and practice takes time. The pressures of modern family life offer precious little time for parents to work on their own skills of self-calming unless they realize how important it is and set aside time for practice.

The parent whose emotional life is influenced by alcohol, drugs, mental illness, or extreme stress so that healthy self-calming is all but impossible will have difficulty accepting the need for this practice until the consequences of their ineffective behavior become clear to them. But many who have chosen to participate in a program of recovery from alcohol, drugs, depression, or violence have learned the importance of such programs. They have found support systems that help and made the necessary time for them.

This chapter cannot hope to provide guidelines for all the complexities of shame and anger that occur in family life. Shame and anger show up in parent child interactions throughout the development of the child, from infancy to independence and frequently beyond. Recognizing this may make it clear how important it is for parents to define and actively practice healthy emotional skills.

An Infant's Experience of Shame

Kaufman believes the facial expression of shame can be noticed in infancy at the moment when the adoring gaze of the nursing mother is interrupted and the bonding of mother and child interrupted along with it.[47] It is certainly possible to evoke the mild distress and averted gaze of shame by staring at

Implications for Parenting

a young baby with an aggressive frown. Fortunately, babies are resilient, and they are able to release feelings of shame and anger quickly in howls of distress, then respond to smiles of reconciliation or affection with coos and giggles. If the parent is very distracted, emotionally troubled, or absent a lot, the soothing, affectionate bonding process is interrupted, and seeds of insecurity may take root in the child at a very young age.

Babies can also be frightened by the sounds of anger if parents are fighting or scolding older children and may experience sympathetic shame and distress. There is a delicate period at around eighteen months for many babies when separation anxiety becomes a potential problem. The child is more aware of the parent's coming and going, and it is the going that creates the anxiety.

The time honored game of peekaboo is an appropriate activity at this stage. When a parent hides her face, and then emerges with a smile, parent and baby are practicing an early form of time out, practicing the rhythm of shame and reconciliation. The parent "goes away," if only behind her hands or a blanket, then "comes back" with a reassuring smile. If the parent "goes away" for too long during this age of separation anxiety, the gaze of curious anticipation on the baby's face will rapidly turn to distress and tears.

Shame and Toilet Training

It is perfectly understandable that parents soon grow tired of dirty diapers and look forward to the time when a child can be toilet trained before the child is even capable of the sphincter control necessary for this developmental milestone. Before the child is motivated for or capable of this task, he will have heard enough comments about "yucky," "dirty," or "nasty" messes to have begun to associate a certain degree of disapproval with the whole business. Since there is nothing the child can do about it until he reaches a specific stage of physical maturation, he can well feel blame or shame over something he cannot control. This can lead to avoidance behavior such as denying a wet or dirty diaper when asked, which may bring more expressions of parental disapproval. This tension can plant the seed of a power struggle over toilet training when the time is finally right.

One of the keys to minimizing such struggles is knowing when it is appropriate to expect a child to be ready for toilet training and recognizing the cues that he is beginning to be motivated to learn this skill. Most children will not be capable of the necessary sphincter control before the age of two, so that parental expectations of toilet training before that will only generate frustration and failure.

Once the child is capable, there is the matter of motivation. Is the child going to try to use the potty because he wants to please the parent, avoid disapproval, or experience pride in his own self-mastery? Of these three, the motivation for self-mastery is the strongest and least likely to lead to power struggles. At this stage of life, children are highly motivated to learn to do new things for themselves as long as the new skills are within their ability. By contrast, learning to do something because parents want it or in order to avoid parental disapproval are more complicated motivations, and tend to come into conflict with the child's motivation for self-mastery and self-determination.

Three year old Elizabeth's mother had plenty of evidence that she was capable of using the potty regularly, but Elizabeth showed no interest in any of her mother's inducements to do so. Mom began to think she was just being stubborn and to wonder whether it was an indication of other developmental problems she should be worried about. Elizabeth was highly motivated to begin preschool, however, having an older brother already in school. When Mom mentioned that Elizabeth needed to be able to use the potty herself when she went to school because the teachers did not have time to change diapers, Elizabeth trained herself within days.

Shame and Anger and the "Terrible Twos"

Toddlers have a reputation for being difficult. They are just beginning to discover their own power after having survived the discovery that they are separate from, and yet dependent upon,

Implications for Parenting

their parents. They are learning how to say "NO!" and how to express their own opinions. This brings them into conflict with others, almost all of whom are bigger and more powerful than they are. This results in many defeats. The emotions of shame and anger are frequently exercised and practiced, and patterns of emotional behavior are shaped during the constant repetition of experiments with power and defeat.

It is impossible to protect children from defeats, shame, and anger in early life, but even if it were possible, it would be inadvisable. Just as children need to learn how to assert themselves and prevail, they also need to learn to assert themselves and accept defeats. Most of all, they need to learn to tolerate the relevant emotions in the relatively safe environment of the family in much the same way that tiger cubs learn to use their claws and teeth by wrestling with their siblings and attempting to ambush their mother. The parent who understands the power of the interplay between shame and anger and reconciliation is better prepared to help the toddler learn to negotiate the defeats without excessive shame or anger.

Little Sean wanted to go back to the "fun jungle" at the zoo when it was time for lunch. He would not accept no from his grandfather and thrashed with all his strength until he was put down. He ran several steps toward the fun jungle but grandfather did not follow. Sean turned and loudly demanded to be taken to the fun jungle, but his grandfather just watched and waited from about twenty feet away. Sean stamped his feet in a puddle, got red in the face from screaming for his parents who were not with them, and repeatedly insisted on being taken to the fun jungle. At an earlier time in his life, grandfather might have become ashamed and angry at this public display, but experience had taught him patience. After about three minutes of this, Sean was tired and realized it wasn't getting him anywhere. He lifted his arms up and said, "Grandpa, will you carry me?" And his grandfather said, "OK, if you will come to me." Sean resignedly trudged the twenty feet to where Grandpa was standing and was lifted up and carried off to lunch.

Chapter Eleven

The "time out" technique of disciplining a young child is popular and effective because it uses the normal dynamics of shame and reconciliation flexibly to discipline and reward. At the same time, it can help teach self-calming. When a young child is placed on time out as a sign of disapproval, the length of the time out can be very short, because the attention span of a young child is very short. As soon as the child experiences the withholding of approval and attention, and shows some signs of wanting reconciliation, the time out has done its job. The time out can then be ended in exchange for a small behavioral change by the child. The behavioral change should be something simple and well within the child's ability in order to avoid creating another failure situation. And the behavior can be designed to teach self-calming. "Can you take three long slow breaths?" or "Let me see you stretch as tall as you can three times." Part of the goal of the time out is to interrupt the emotional state that may have precipitated it and demonstrate to the child that he can change the emotion and behavior that led to the time out. When these simple expectations are repeated, the child soon remembers the self-calming procedure as the key to ending the time out and is better prepared to listen to more expectations about solving the problem that led to the time out.

Parents who are unaware of or insensitive to the power and dynamics of shame and anger are at risk of leaving the child in the tension of shame too long, thereby generating more anger and more defiant behavior. Parents who are too concerned with winning the power struggle or expressing their own anger are likely to inadvertently create an environment where shame and anger dominate and the power of reconciliation is diminished. For a toddler, a minute or two of disapproval is a long time. Often 30 seconds is sufficient—and much more easily enforced.

Some parents have expressed concern over what they consider the calculated emotional manipulation of children in these techniques. My response to this is that all socialization involves the emotional manipulation of children in order to motivate them to accept social norms. A conscious effort based on sensitivity to and understanding of the primary emotional dynamics is much less likely to become abusive. Establishing a

Implications for Parenting

pattern of mild emotional discipline through the withholding of attention in a time out accomplishes two things. It offers the expectation of reconciliation early in the child's experience, reinforcing the sense of safety that builds self-esteem. It also allows that expectation to be used effectively to motivate the child to accept and learn appropriate behaviors and problem solving approaches throughout childhood. Failure to set limits and establish the pattern of expectations early on leads to a situation in which the child's behavior forces a confrontation sooner or later. The parent may then have to resort to more forceful interventions because the older undisciplined child is harder to control. If the parent then feels guilty about losing control or using excessive force, the interplay of anger, guilt, and more anger between parent and child begins to take root in a disturbing way.

Let us try to shine some light on why shame makes the parenting job more difficult and some of the developmental issues most likely to involve shame. A special problem stems from the fact that shame naturally compels us to hide—to withdraw from the field of conflict—to seek to become invisible. This explains why it is natural for a child to hide or deny a mistake as part of the shame response to anticipated parental disapproval. Have you noticed how early and how appropriately many children learn to pronounce that simple and telling phrase, "Uh oh!"

When a child denies responsibility for muddy tracks or a broken vase, parents often interpret this as lying and attribute it to the child's fear of punishment or at least fear of the parent's anger. The instinct to hide in response to shame is not as well understood as the instinct to hide in response to fear. When the parent is not expressing anger, he may be confused about the child's avoidance behavior. When the child then shows some angry behavior, the aggressive phase of the shame/anger response, parents may interpret it as willful defiance. When the parent repeatedly labels this anger as defiance, the child learns to understand it this way as well, even though she knows at some level it isn't really willful. Teaching a child to label and understand his own feelings is a complex job. Teaching about

147

shame and anger is further complicated by the fact that we don't like to talk about shame and don't understand it very well. The shame is hidden and poorly understood, but the anger is visible, and we understand the function of anger better. We just don't understand the relationship between the two.

Four year old Timmy was climbing up on the counter to get a cookie when he accidentally knocked a casserole dish to the floor, breaking it. His twenty month old brother standing in the doorway pronounced a distinct "Uh oh!" Timmy's embarrassed distress shifted quickly to irritation at his brother, and Mom arrived on the scene just in time to hear Timmy hissing, "Shut up, stupid!"

It would be tempting for Mom to comfort the tearful baby while scolding Timmy for 1) trying to sneak a cookie without permission, 2) breaking the casserole, and 3) calling his brother a name. But this mom was alert and emotionally intelligent and recognized that this teaching opportunity was worth more than cookies or casseroles.

While calming the baby, she asked, "Timmy, are you ok?" Timmy somewhat sullenly agreed that he was. Mom said, "Come on out here away from the broken glass. We'll clean that up later." She quickly moved on to talking about feelings.

"I'll bet you didn't mean to break the casserole, and you felt bad about it when it happened. Is that right?" Timmy agreed, cautiously.

"It's normal to feel bad when you have an accident or make a mistake, even if you couldn't help it, but even more so if you think it was your fault. And you know what else is normal?"

Timmy, curious about the direction of this conversation, but still cautious, said no, he didn't know what else.

"Right after we feel bad about an accident or a mistake, we get mad—even when there is no reason to be angry. It's just a normal part of the bad feeling after we make a mistake or get disappointed. Sometimes we get mad at ourselves and sometimes we get mad at somebody else for no reason. That's probably why you called Jake stupid."

Implications for Parenting

Timmy prepares for the consequences he suspects are about to be announced, but is surprised when Mom moves on.

"I know I say things I don't mean when I'm mad sometimes, and they may hurt your feelings—which is why it's important to talk about feelings. Do you understand what I am talking about?"

Timmy looked uncertain, but nodded cooperatively.

"That's ok," said Mom. "We'll talk about it again sometime. Now will you help me to clean up the broken casserole?"

Timmy eagerly agreed to this, sensing a chance for reconciliation, not knowing that it was his own shame and anger that threatened to exile him in this situation.

By taking this calm and reasoned approach, Mom has sown a seed for future understanding of complex emotions. By reading stories in which a character feels some shame and anger, she can refer back to this event to help Timmy understand the normality of his feelings, the importance of calming anger and seeking reconciliation where possible, and techniques for doing so.

This is an ambitious undertaking considering all that parents have to juggle in family life. But the rewards of emotional intelligence are great, and the consequences of leaving our children to face life at the mercy of powerful and confusing emotions are potentially dire. The teaching process can be broken down into lots of little steps, and parents can learn more as they teach. They may even learn from their children.

One mother of a four year old boy who was having regular tantrums provoked by jealousy of his younger sister taught him a simple deep breathing technique to help him calm down when he was upset. She praised him for trying it and prompted him to use it a few times to recover from a meltdown. A week later, she was driving the family van with both kids in the back seat, and she overheard her four year old teaching the breathing technique to his younger sister. A week after that, when she was frazzled and upset, both children came to her, patting her reassuringly and coaching, "Breathe, Mommy, breathe!"

Teasing and Bullying: Shame on the Playground

When children begin to attend school, they encounter a world full of emotional dangers and many opportunities to feel powerless. Some children may already have experienced teasing and bullying from siblings at home. This may account for a tendency to establish themselves in the larger world of the school peer group by using teasing or bullying as a preemptive strike against shaming by others. Other victims of teasing or bullying at home may find their victim role confirmed and reinforced by teasing experiences at school. And some cheerful and confident children may encounter teasing and bullying for the first time in the social competition of the peer group and be unprepared for it. They will almost certainly react with shame and anger that they do not know how to express or resolve.

If a child has not already learned how to recover from shame and anger fairly quickly, he may be in for a crash course. Before long, he will encounter a competitive peer or a disapproving adult who will trigger feelings of shame and helplessness, followed by feelings of aggression or even rage. He will practice one or more emotional strategies for dealing with this situation and choose one as his favorite. He may try to bury the anger by taking it out on himself in a damaging flurry of self-criticism. He may fantasize revenge and even plan and execute some form of retaliation. He may take his aggression out on someone else, seeking a way to restore status by teasing or harassing another, or by shifting blame. Or he may find a supportive listener with whom to work out this problem, though this requires skill and sensitive communication from the child and the listener. There are so many such episodes in his young life that a preference for one of the strategies is soon established. It may work well enough in the short term to hide the helplessness and take the shame inside, or to gain back a sense of power by shaming another. But often it may result in some unreleased shame or anger that grows into a chronic expectation of social danger.

Implications for Parenting

The parent who does not expect his child to be sorely tested by teasing and bullying may resort to the conventional advice, "Just ignore it." Or an active parent may seek to confront the problem for his child by talking to the teacher or the parents of the bully. Organized efforts to fight systemic teasing and bullying have been tried in individual schools—and even the entire school system in Norway. Similar efforts in elementary schools in the U.S. were reported in an article on "NO PUT DOWN" zones in The Washington Post.[48] The "No Put Down" Program was created by a non-profit organization in Syracuse, NY that has generated a manual used in elementary schools to help parents and teachers work together to teach character building skills to students. These efforts have demonstrated some success, but are very difficult to maintain, requiring the consistent participation and cooperation of parents, teachers, and administrators in sustaining a program to confront a problem that has its roots in our emotional wiring. We have to face the fact that shame and anger are part of our evolutionary heritage and will tend to show up in social competition among children. It is even more likely to show up among adolescents when the importance of a secure place in the peer group becomes a developmental priority.

One of the best things we can do is to teach our children how to recognize and handle the emotions stirred up in this process and encourage them in problem solving efforts that they can discuss with us as they face this challenging emotional environment. There have been several books written about teasing and bullying with specific tips for coping. These books tend to agree that listening respectfully to the child's struggles and respecting their own ways of solving them is better than trying to tell them what to do, and much better than telling them simply to ignore the harassment. The latter approach tends to minimize the child's problem and make them think there is no use trying to talk to you about it. One of the things that makes listening difficult in these situations is the fact that most children will be tempted to hide the shame of bullying. That is part of the nature of shame. So parents need to be alert to signs of this dilemma and look for constructive ways to invite their child to talk about it, showing respect for the power of the feelings and encouraging brainstorming about ways to deal with the situation. The model described in How to Talk so Kids Will Listen and Listen So Kids Will Talk, by Adel Faber and Elaine Mazlish[49] is useful in this kind of problem solving conversation. If the stage has been set by establishing a language for talking about feelings, including shame or hurt feelings and anger, the conversation will flow more smoothly.

"Mistakes" and the Young Child

A Bedtime Story

Once upon a time there was a boy who made a mistake. At least he thought it was a mistake. He left his new jacket out on the playground after a soccer game and, when he went back to get it, it was gone. To be honest, it was not the first time he had made a mistake. And perhaps it wasn't the worst mistake he could have made. But he felt truly terrible about it.

He felt terrible even before he saw the irritated look on his mother's face. He felt terrible even before his father asked him how he could be so careless. It was an immediate terrible feeling as soon as he realized what had happened. He was too young to know in any meaningful way that everyone makes mistakes and that almost everyone feels some version of the terrible feeling when they do. He was too young to know that the name of the terrible feeling was shame and that it was often triggered by making mistakes. He was just beginning to learn the concept of failure that is associated with shame and mistakes, but it was just a vague idea and a bad feeling at this point.

The following weekend, when his mother told him it was time to go buy a new jacket, he said he didn't want to go. He felt angry, partly at the person who had taken his jacket and partly at himself for being so stupid and forgetting it in the first place. He was too young to know that the angry feelings are part of the natural reaction to shame that follows a big

Implications for Parenting

disappointment or mistake. In his anger, he was so stubborn that his mother decided not to force the issue by dragging him to the store against his will. His father thought it would teach him a lesson to go without a jacket for a while.

The next day, he refused go to soccer. He knew his parents liked seeing him play soccer. He always had fun at it. But he was still angry over the lost jacket and he didn't feel like playing. He felt like a failure and even went so far as to say "I'm no good at soccer," although he knew he was better than many of the kids on his team. He was too young to know that shame and anger can become attached to a lot of things besides the event that triggered them in the first place. He didn't know how close he was coming to developing the habit of feeling ashamed and angry about more and more things until he felt that way about himself all the time.

That night he was still feeling upset when his father came in to read a story to him and his little brother. They were reading "The Sword and the Stone" again and were at one of his favorite parts, where Merlin is teaching young Wart the magic arts. Wart is a clumsy youth who makes plenty of mistakes, but always seems to get away with no harm done. The boy fell asleep thinking that it wasn't fair that he should end up feeling so bad about his jacket. And then he had a remarkable dream.

In his dream, he went back to the soccer field to look for his jacket. It wasn't anywhere on the field. Next to the field there were some bushes, and he decided to look further. Just beyond the bushes he found a path into a forest that was dark and kind of mysterious. It made him a little scared but he still wanted to look for the jacket, so he kept going. It got darker and darker, but just when he was about to turn back, he saw a lighter place down the path. There he found a sunny clearing and in the middle of the clearing, was a large gray boulder with something that looked like an old rusty sword sticking out of the middle of it.

He approached the boulder with wonder and a little fear, but the sword seemed to fade and disappear as he got close to it. He was walking around staring at the spot where the sword

Chapter Eleven

should have been when suddenly he was startled halfway out of his sneakers by a loud and cheerful, "Hello!"

He spun around, terrified, to see an old man in a purple robe with a long white beard striding into the clearing.

"Oh dear, did I frighten you? I'm so sorry," he said. "Darn! I'm always making mistakes like that."

"Are you Merlin?" the boy asked in a shaky voice.

"Why, yes! How did you know?" said Merlin.

"I read a book—or my father read us a book. I just guessed," answered the boy.

"That was a pretty good guess," said Merlin. "Say, you haven't seen a bag of charms anywhere around here, have you? I left it somewhere by mistake."

"No," said the boy. "Sorry."

"It's very irritating to lose things, isn't it?"

"I know," said the boy. "I lost my jacket."

"Did you really?" said Merlin. "I'll bet it made you feel terrible."

"Uh huh!"

"I had a young friend who used to feel terrible about mistakes until I told him there was no better way to learn."

"What do you mean?"

"I mean that if you do things perfectly, there is nothing to learn. When you make a mistake, you can improve if you are willing to admit it and think about it."

"But no one likes to admit making mistakes," said the boy.

"Aye - there's the rub. People don't like it because they are afraid someone will look down on them, so they don't think about mistakes the way they should in order to learn from them."

"How is that?"

"Very simple. You ask yourself, 'if I could do this over again what would I do differently?' Usually you come up with some ideas. If not, you can watch other people and notice what they do. Or ask them."

Implications for Parenting

"But aren't people embarrassed to make mistakes?"

"Yes they are. Such a shame. It's a bad habit—feeling embarrassed about mistakes, but anyone can get over that habit if they want to."

"How?"

"Practice! If you practice making mistakes everyday and thinking of ways you could improve, pretty soon you will start feeling good about many of your mistakes, especially if you congratulate yourself on what you learn."

"I wish I could learn that" said the boy.

"You can learn it! Just as easily as learning to spell 'prestidigitation.' You may have to break it down into parts at first, but soon you can pull it all together."

"I don't know if I can do that."

"I do. I'll bet you a bag of magic charms that if you follow my instructions and do your homework, you will find out how to learn from your mistakes without feeling bad about them."

"Homework! I have to do homework?"

"Of course! Your homework is to make two mistakes a day, three for extra credit. And at night, congratulate yourself for your mistakes and go right to sleep to dream up some ways to learn from them. In the morning, try to talk to someone about what you learned from yesterday's mistakes."

"Can I count any mistakes?"

"Certainly. Big or small. Even ones nobody knows about but you."

"What if I can't dream up any way to learn from my mistakes?"

"Then you might want to talk to your parents, or a teacher, or even a friend."

"My parents might be mad if I tell them about some mistakes."

"Maybe, but they'll soon get over it, and if you tell them you are trying to learn from your mistakes, they'll probably be a lot less upset. Will you give it a try?"

Chapter Eleven

"Okay," said the boy.

"Good, I must go now, because it is almost time for you to wake up. Here, just follow this firefly out of the forest."

And with that, Merlin pulled a very large firefly out of his pocket and threw it into the air. It began to lead the way back down the path toward the soccer field. The boy followed it, and when he looked back toward the clearing, Merlin was waving goodbye.

"I'll be here if you need to chat again sometime."

The boy began to wave back, when he thought to ask Merlin about the sword. But before he could speak Merlin disappeared in a large puff of white smoke, and the boy woke up in his own bed.

He was quiet at breakfast, but before leaving for school, he told his mother, "I've been thinking about how to remember my jacket in the future, and I've decided to put all my things together on the side of the field closest to home, so I'll be sure to see them when I pass on the way home. That way I won't forget them when I leave."

"That's very wise," said his mother, clearly impressed.

The boy felt so good about this that he told her, "I guess it's okay to go shopping for another jacket now."

And they did.

All parents would love for their children to learn from mistakes. Most of us would like our children to learn from <u>our</u> mistakes, but it doesn't seem to work that way. Children have to determine for themselves that they have made a mistake, and they are much more likely to learn from it if they are challenged to solve the problem themselves, with a little help. Children begin to strive for independence before they can balance on two feet. They like to solve problems themselves whenever possible and are less enchanted with (and less likely to remember) an answer that is handed to them by others.

Implications for Parenting

Parents operate under the pressures of time and great expectations. It is understandable that they want to give children the answer rather than encouraging them to learn from their mistakes by thinking them through. Thinking through a situation and developing a solution or alternative takes time for adults and children, though children can sometimes surprise you with their creative insights. Often a parent is in too much of a hurry for the child to "get it right." In our haste, we may reject their efforts to solve their own problems and offer them our solutions instead. This rejection stimulates shame and anger, and often a rejection of the solution that the parent offers.

If the child naturally begins to associate mistakes with shame, he will be highly motivated to hide mistakes by lying, forgetting, or minimizing them, rather than thinking about possible solutions. If talking about mistakes is a painful, shaming experience, the child will not want our help in figuring out better solutions. One alternative for parents is to make a determined effort to legitimize mistakes and to celebrate creative thinking about solutions.

The story is told of an accomplished scientist who attributed his successful work habits to his mother's attitudes toward mistakes. He gave this example. At age 4, he was attempting to pour himself a glass of milk, when the bottle slipped and milk spilled all over the kitchen floor.

His mother, hearing the noise, came to the kitchen door, and exclaimed, "Goodness! What a lovely milk spill! Would you like to play with it for awhile before we clean it up?" She then joined her son in building little dams and rivers of milk on the kitchen floor for a few minutes and then suggested several ways they could clean up the milk, asking his opinion about which would work best.

After having carefully cleaned the floor together, she suggested that they take the empty milk bottle out into the back yard, fill it with water, and practice different ways of holding, carrying and pouring it that would be easy for 4-year-old hands. While he was busy with that, she asked him if he would like her to pour him a glass of milk or would he rather do it

Chapter Eleven

himself. He was happy to have her pour it for him, especially since she had given him the choice.

Many parents react to this story with skepticism, worrying that this standard of acceptance of mistakes would require more time and patience than it is reasonable to expect in the normal modern family. While this skepticism is understandable, it should also be noted that becoming angry and getting into a power struggle with a child over mistakes also takes a great deal of time and generates a great deal of stress in the process. It also adds to a pattern of shame, resentment, and frustration associated with mistakes.

Some families decide to make a family game or ritual out of recognizing mistakes and their potential for learning. In order for this to work, parents must be willing to report and admit their own mistakes as well as asking their children to do so. Shaming, blaming, or teasing about mistakes is against the rules, and having the courage to admit a mistake is praised. Advice about solutions is discouraged unless it is asked for, and almost all potential solutions are accepted as initial possibilities.

The model for collaborative problem solving is described in the Faber and Mazlish book.[50] Accepting all of the child's potential solutions is often challenging for parents because children often come up with solutions that seem silly, unrealistic, or undesirable to parents. But accepting all potential solutions is consistent with the creative process of brainstorming, where critical judgment is suspended in the generation of ideas. After a list of potential solutions is generated, no matter how wild some of them may seem to be, the choice of the best on the list can be based on an understanding of reality, consequences, and resources. If Johnny imagines that one awesome solution to the mistake of getting into a fight at school would be to move to Hawaii, information about the costs of such a move would have to enter into the discussion.

Implications for Parenting

Shame in Adolescence

Adolescence is a time in life ripe with opportunities for shame. It is a time when belonging in your peer group while standing out as someone special are both extremely important yet often contradictory goals. The rules are changing, bodies are changing, and everything is happening quickly. It is also a time when the young person is redefining himself as a more independent individual. There is a risk of shame issues taking root in the evolving self-image of the adolescent that will have repercussions for years to come. Sexual feelings and encounters are unavoidable, highly charged, and simultaneously exciting and scary. But emotionally charged attitudes toward sex are established much earlier.

When Jared was four, he was playing with some blocks and toy figures when his father asked him about the fantasy action. "The tiger is chasing the princess," he reported.

"What happens when he catches her?"

"He'll marry her," came the answer.

"What do they do then?" Dad asked.

"They go to the bedroom."

"What do they do in the bedroom?"

"Oh Dad," Jared blurted out. "That's the embarrassing part!"

Children learn early on that sex is private and that talking about it or even thinking about it can be shameful or embarrassing. Adults, in their efforts to teach children about socially acceptable norms, convey the idea that sexual play and exploration is improper, or perhaps dirty or evil. In response, most children suppress or sublimate sexual curiosity for a period of time between early childhood and puberty. The interim period is called "latency age" in child development texts because the sexual drive and behavior appear to be latent until the hormonal changes and social pressures of early adolescence make it all but impossible to suppress. But sexual awareness and curiosity is not absent, even in latency age children.

159

Chapter Eleven

Children know that sexual matters are taboo for them and they experience shame, embarrassment, or guilt about their own sexual curiosity or sensations.

Ritchie was watching a PG rated movie with his parents when a sexually suggestive scene made him feel acutely embarrassed, imagining that his parents would know what he was thinking. He pretended he had to go to the toilet and left the theater until the scene was over.

Angie discovered the secret pleasures of masturbation at age eight and felt terribly guilty about it. She considered it as final proof that she was a bad person. She made a vow to stop, but when she could not resist, she became convinced that she would someday have to atone for this sin.

Then puberty happens, and the young person is simultaneously stimulated by hormonal changes, changes in her own body, and changes in the bodies of her peers. Social competition takes on a new intensity and teasing carries a quality of sexual innuendo.

There are two periods in life during which brain cells and synaptic connections grow rapidly. Both are associated with rapid physical and mental development. The first period is during the child's first two years of life when he is learning to move and control his body and to communicate. The second period is during adolescence, when the young person is experiencing rapid growth and sexual development and is learning to function socially and sexually. He is exercising and expanding his independence and self-reliance. Emotional growth is also taking place as he experiences new emotions and learns to manage them. The young person is learning to deal with excitement, embarrassment, anger, anxiety, and sexual drives at the same time he is learning independence—and therefore he must learn about these things more or less on his own. Because shame compels us to hide, it intensifies the need for privacy and secrecy for an adolescent. Confusion and misinformation are more difficult to correct when communication is hampered by privacy concerns or shame.

Implications for Parenting

The prevalence of shame about the discussion of these matters makes it difficult for most adolescents to ask questions in order to correct confusion or misinformation. It takes a skillful and sensitive parent to create an atmosphere in which questions can be asked. When secret shame about sexual feelings goes unchecked in an adolescent's private world, there is potential for toxic shame to shape and warp the young person's self-esteem.

Confusion and shame over sexuality are painful experiences for almost everyone at some point in adolescence, and sometimes these feelings are further complicated by societal attitudes intended to suppress premature sexual activity. Frank McCourt, in his memoir, Angela's Ashes,[51] gives a vivid account of an adolescent boy's agonizing struggle with sexual curiosity and its conflict with the fearful spiritual consequences of "impure thoughts" as taught in the strict Roman Catholic culture of Limerick, Ireland where he grew up.

Sexual education that includes information about the emotions associated with sex, including the role of shame and embarrassment, may help avoid some of the potentially toxic misunderstandings that can begin in adolescence.

Criticism and the Challenge of Independence.

As adolescents strive for independence, differentiating themselves from their parents and their own childhood reliance on parents and other significant adults, they encounter criticism on all sides. They can expect criticism from teachers and parents as they try out their independence, sometimes in rebellious or defiant behaviors. They can also expect criticism from their peers, sometimes through teasing and bullying or through subtle but powerful ostracism, and sometimes through direct confrontation. Criticism, of course, evokes a shame / anger reaction. But by the time the adolescent faces criticism, he has already developed a clear tendency either to resign himself to any judgment or to angrily reject any criticism. Sometimes this tendency is so well established in the early teen years that it is difficult to convince an adolescent that he has the choice and the responsibility to decide for himself what criticism to accept and what to reject.

Some parents cannot respect the adolescent's ability to make his own decisions and his need to exercise and practice this responsibility. The parent then insists on the right to make the decision and the adolescent withdraws in shame. When this happens, the opportunity for instructive dialogue is lost, seeds of anger and defiance are sown, and the field of constructive criticism between parent and adolescent shrinks and becomes polarized.

Todd complained to his counselor that his father was never satisfied with anything he did. He admitted that he had made mistakes and had gotten into some pretty serious trouble in middle school, but now his father responded to every situation, good or bad, with a litany of reminders of his past failures and predictions that he would fail again. When the counselor suggested that it was time for Todd to begin to decide for himself what was a success and what was a failure, Todd could not understand. "No matter what I think," he said, "my father will never be satisfied. He always has to prove me wrong." The counselor told him that as long as he depended on his father's approval, he would be trapped. But Todd could neither let go of the shame of his past mistakes, nor his anger at his father.

If children can be taught how to process criticism without the damaging emotional swings of shame and anger, if parents and children both understand how to keep these normal emotions from undermining healthy communication—then parents and children alike will have an easier time of it.

The long period of development from infancy to independence provides many opportunities to teach emotional intelligence skills to deal with shame and anger. No one can be perfectly consistent in dealing with these powerful feelings or teaching them. But we can practice. If we recognize the high stakes at risk, and we practice and teach as diligently as we can, we can share our own growing awareness and emotional intelligence with the next generation. In this way, though the

Implications for Parenting

brains we evolved in more primitive times will not have changed, we will continue to evolve, by adding skills that are culturally transmitted from one generation to the next.

Recommended Books on Parenting

How to Talk So Kids Will Listen & Listen So Kids Will Talk by Adele Faber and Elaine Mazlish, Quill Books, 1980.

Kids Are Worth It by Barbara Coloroso, Somerville House, 1994.

Raising Your Spirited Child by Mary Sheedy Kurcinka, HarperCollins, 1991.

Becoming the Parent You Want to Be by Laura Davis and Janis Keyser, Broadway Books, 1997.

It's Not Fair: Jeremy Spencer's Parents Let Him Stay up all Night by Anthony E. Wolf, Noonday, 1995.

Positive Discipline for Teenagers by Jane Nelsen and Lynn Lott, Prima Publishing, 2000.

Section Three

Shame and Anger
in the
Human Condition

Chapter Twelve

Shame and Loss

Criticism, as we have seen, is experienced throughout life, potentially triggering reactions of shame and anger unless we can master these reactions and turn the experience of receiving criticism to our advantage. But the linked affects of shame and anger are not limited to the experience of criticism.

A major thesis of this book has been that the experience of shame is hardwired to the subsequent experience of anger; that the two sequential affects—first shame, then anger—occur almost universally in humans and other species in response to negative or threatening stimuli. A combination this powerful is too strong not to play a role in our lives well beyond that of receiving criticism. These primary emotional responses can be evoked by any real or perceived defeat, disappointment,

Chapter Twelve

reversal, or loss in the course of a lifetime. They permeate our societies and the way we view and function in the communities in which we live. They impact the great and historic institutions that run the world—governments, religious institutions, national cooperation or rivalry—to mention only a few. They are very much a part of the full scope of the human condition and must be considered in any attempt to understand ourselves and how we live together with others.

In this section of the book we will briefly look at three additional and important aspects of the shame/anger connection: our response to the major losses in our lives; the institutional and societal manifestations of shame and anger that impact all of us; and the spiritual connection to our hardwired biological imperative.

Loss

The normal or predictable response to one of life's most painful realities, the experience of grief, is similar to depression. The connections we have made between shame and depression may also help us understand the storm of emotions that we must endure in the response to a significant loss.

The serenity prayer, composed by Dr. Reinhold Niebuhr in 1932 and memorized by millions in self-help recovery programs, begins, "God give me the serenity to accept things that cannot be changed..." Of the many things we cannot change, the most poignant are the irreversible losses we suffer throughout life. We are deeply and firmly attached to our families, friends, homes, preferences, talents, toys, stories, and dreams. We never want to give up any of the people, things, and ideas we love, depend on, or even take for granted. But it is inevitable that we must.

A young mother who had lost her baby went to the wise woman who lived on the edge of the forest looking for a cure for her agonizing grief. The wise woman told her, "Take this empty bowl. Go to the homes of all the families in the village who have not lost a child and ask for rice. When the bowl is full, bring it back to me and you will have the cure for your pain."

The young mother went to every house in the town and returned to the wise woman with the bowl still empty. She had found no family that had not lost a child. But in her search, she found compassion—the compassion shown to her by others and the compassion she felt for them.

We suffer loss and we grieve. Elizabeth Kubler-Ross explained the process of grief in her pioneering work <u>On Death and Dying</u> in 1969.[52] In it she lists and explores the five stages of grief: 1) denial, 2) anger, 3) bargaining, 4) depression, and 5) acceptance. At that time, Kubler-Ross was researching the emotional stages of individuals diagnosed with a terminal illness, but these stages also proved to be applicable to grieving the loss of a loved one, a home, a dream, or indeed, anything of deep personal value to an individual. These five stages are now familiar to everyone working in health or mental health fields, as well as to many in the general public.

The victim of sudden death does not, as far as we know, have time to experience this sequence of emotional reactions. But an individual diagnosed with a terminal illness does have time, as do those who survive the death of a loved one. In the years since Dr. Kubler-Ross formulated these five stages of grief they have been studied and applied to all kinds of significant losses to help us understand our normal reactions to loss. What has not been directly addressed in the body of literature on loss and grief is the role of shame and its connection to the early phases of the grief process.

If we think of a significant loss as a kind of defeat, it may bring the role of shame more clearly into focus. The person who has lost a loved one to death has been both defeated and robbed. If he had the power to prevent this he would have done so. Confronted by such a loss he finds himself powerless and bereft. This is a condition that evokes shame in the fundamental way we have discussed it, as a reaction to defeat. It is not embarrassment or a moral judgment, but a withdrawal following defeat, hiding in the face of an overwhelming opponent.

Chapter Twelve

Kubler-Ross calls the first stage of grief "denial and isolation." This suggests similarities to the hiding and withdrawal of the shame response. In defeat and shame, we withdraw from the conflict, averting our eyes, masking our aggression, and doing what we can to make ourselves and our shame invisible. In the first stage of grief, we recoil in shock and denial, unable to face the truth, unwilling to expose ourselves to the full impact of the loss. We delay and deny and pretend that we don't have to accept loss yet. So perhaps the first phase of grief can be understood as the instinctive shame response to an intolerable defeat.

The second stage formulated by Kubler-Ross, that of anger, could then be understood as the automatic aggressive surge that follows the shame response to defeat or loss. Those who study grief have noted that the anger triggered in grief can often be misdirected or inappropriately expressed. Medical staff and other caretakers may become the target of anger over grief they did nothing to cause or aggravate. When there is no appropriate target for the anger, it may be expressed to those who happen to be closest, even other family members who are also struggling with grief. The anger of the grief-stricken can also be confusing to the person experiencing and expressing it. If we expect rational explanations for the anger that flows out of grief, we will be confounded and disoriented. If, on the other hand, we think of it as an automatic response, a part of the hardwired shame/anger response to defeat and loss, we may be better able to accept, understand, and forgive some of the grief-generated anger.

The third or "bargaining" phase formulated by Dr. Kubler-Ross describes a complex phenomenon that is difficult to understand in psychological terms. With whom is the grieving person bargaining? And for what? A man diagnosed with a terminal illness may think, "If this diagnosis can be reversed, I will promise to live a better life." The father of a sick child may make a silent promise, "If my child is spared, I will never raise my voice to her again." Such bargaining with God or fate seems to take place even when the bargainer does not believe in the possibility that the outcome will be affected. This phase is also seen in the "survivor guilt" expressed by those who grieve and often wish to be given another chance in the relationship with the lost loved one. The desperation that underlies the bargaining phase is quite compelling. But there may be some insight to be gained from recalling the primal function of shame and anger and applying this to the understanding of the bargaining phase of grief.

A defeated animal surrenders and withdraws in shame, avoiding obliteration. But it is soon compelled by an instinctive surge of aggression to assert itself again into the field of competition to find a place in the hierarchy of survivors. If the next opponent also defeats it, the cycle is repeated, the animal withdraws, then rebounds, until it finds an opponent it can defeat, whereupon it assumes its place in the natural hierarchy.

The victim of loss is similarly rocked by shame and helplessness, but is instinctively compelled to fight back, to hope for a miracle, to offer promise if threat cannot win the prize. We cannot tolerate helplessness for long without seeking some way to win. But there is no winning against the finality of some losses. The grieving person is driven back and forth by shame and anger so that he appears to be fighting, or bargaining, with an invisible opponent.

Eventually, he is exhausted by the struggle, and lapses into a passive state of survival for a while. This is the fourth stage, the one Dr. Kubler-Ross recognizes as the depression phase, when the individual ceases—for a time—to fight. Depression plays a role in allowing the individual to rest from fighting as we have discussed in Chapter 7.

Finally, the individual finds a way to accept a new reality, whether it is the terminally ill patient who finds peace before death or the survivor who finds her way through the labyrinth of grief and is able to accept the loss and move on.

We can find examples of shame and anger playing out in massive public losses and private individual ones throughout life. How each individual navigates the rough waters of grief depends on many factors contributing to her personal resilience.

Chapter Twelve

But if we look closely, the emotional reactions of shame and anger can be found in response to every significant loss.

Shame and Anger in a Disaster

Catastrophic losses of life and property have been an all too regular occurrence in recent times, so it seems appropriate to comment on how shame and anger play out in response to these overwhelming losses. It is not unusual for news coverage on the victims of disaster to emphasize their courage and surprising sense of hope in the immediate aftermath of disasters like September 11th, the Tsunami in Asia, or hurricanes Andrew, Katrina, and Rita. I don't know whether this is because the victims interviewed are experiencing shock and denial or the sense of relief and gratitude that follows a close brush with death. Perhaps these feelings stand out for us as branches of hope to which we can cling in a landscape flooded with despair. I can predict, however, that the grief over catastrophic loss will include the usual suspects, shame and anger, and that if these are ignored they may interfere with recovery. Large scale disasters, where everyone has lost everything, seem to unite us for awhile in a spirit of mutual support, but this admirable condition is temporary. We must understand that a sense of powerlessness triggering shame and anger is the normal response to loss, or we will be caught off balance when these emotions emerge.

When rescue workers arrive with supplies and the best intentions, neither supplies nor good intentions will be enough to assuage the grief, and they may find some of the anger reaction directed towards them. Overwhelmed by the magnitude of the task, they may find themselves also suffering the slings and arrows of shame and anger and may therefore be prey to helper burnout or fatigue sooner. As some stability returns for victims, the magnitude of the loss sinks in and the emotions of grief begin to play out among hundreds of neighbors experiencing the same impact. The sense of overwhelming despair may lead to an increase in suicide as seen in the Gulf states months after hurricane Katrina left hundreds of thousands homeless. Or victims may bond together in expressions of anger that energize them, but can easily be misdirected or unproductive. With the normal fabric of life in shreds and large numbers of grieving individuals interacting with one another, the potential for anger to find outlet in destructive ways is enormous.

Counselors who provide children opportunities to express their fears in drawing pictures and telling stories are trying to give structure to the necessary expression of these feelings. Parents undergoing the same losses, and with the additional burden of powerlessness to protect their children, also need help in expressing, understanding, and resolving their grief. The more active they can be on their own behalf or on behalf of their children, the better able they are to bounce back from disaster. But if left in a powerless limbo for long, they will have to endure the cycle of grief without healthy distraction or outlets for angry energies.

Shame and Disability

Illness or injury that results in a prolonged, progressive, or permanent loss of accustomed abilities precipitates the same sequence of denial and shame, anger, bargaining, and depression before acceptance can provide some peace.

In a scene from the television series "West Wing," President Jed Bartlett denies the shame and limitations imposed by his progressive Multiple Sclerosis and falls in the bathroom, then pounds his legs with his fists in rage. Physical therapists often rely on this anger to mobilize an individual to work hard in rehabilitation exercises, to practice new compensating skills, strengthen atrophied muscles, and adapt to a prosthesis.

Clinicians and family members who underestimate the power of shame and anger in the recently disabled may miss the onset of a dangerous depression in which the victim can see no relief from the shame other than suicide. The young athlete or soldier who suffers a career-ending, life-changing injury plunges from the heights of confidence and ability to the depths of uncertainty and new limitations overnight. Such a cataclysmic personal loss is experienced as a defeat that evokes resounding echoes of shame and anger that may be masked by superficial agreement with assurances offered by family and therapists.

Grief of the same intensity evoked by the loss of a loved one can also be triggered by a partial loss when a loved one is changed or some qualities or abilities that person possessed seem to have been stolen irretrievably. Another television series, "Over There," portraying the experiences of soldiers in the war in Iraq, included the character of a young soldier and former high school football star who loses a leg to an improvised explosive device. His pride in his physical ability and toughness first fuels his denial about the significance of his loss, and he believes he can return to active duty with his unit as soon as he masters the prosthesis. His wife offers reassurances of her love and his importance to her and their baby. But his anger erupts repeatedly, and he insists that they don't know what it is like for him.

She may know more than he suspects because she too has experienced a significant loss. She has lost a physical part of the confident, heroic young husband she married. Though she hopes the emotional change is temporary in some of its aspects, it is a confusing and distressing loss nonetheless, and like every loss, it is experienced as a defeat that triggers shame and anger in the grieving process. Of course it may also be said that she misses the lost leg almost as intimately as he does, but hides her sense of loss to protect him. In a like manner, a husband may grieve following his wife's mastectomy, but try to hide his grief in an attempt to protect her.

When someone suffers from a major mental illness like schizophrenia, Alzheimer's disease, senile dementia, or a major depression, family members experience a progressive loss of the personality they know and love, a loss of the ability to share memories and good times in the way they are accustomed. Because these changes are sometimes intermittent, and therefore confusing, they are even more likely to evoke frustration.

The shame that is a part of grief sometimes manifests as guilt that finds a variety of justifications. There is "survivor guilt" when the grieving person believes it is wrong to continue

Shame and Loss

enjoying life, strength, and wholeness in the face of a partner's loss. Sometimes shame is evoked by empathy with the humiliation of the disabled. Sometimes shame is a reaction to the blast of anger by the suffering partner in response to his own loss, shame, and grief. The dance of shame and anger shared by a couple when one is disabled by illness or injury is not orchestrated for maximum harmony. The expressions of shame and anger by one are easily experienced by the other as criticism or rejection triggering shame and anger in return. It can reflect back and forth instantly like a flash in a hall of mirrors. On the other hand, a partner may suppress anger over a lengthy recuperation leading to burnout and emotional withdrawal.

Shame and Addiction

It is not uncommon for someone struggling with the prolonged or chronic pain of grief or loss to seek relief in drugs or alcohol. Alcohol and painkilling drugs do offer temporary relief for the shame and depression and are known to ease emotional as well as physical pain. But the potential for dependence and addiction provides another arena for the torturous replay of shame and anger. Once a chemical dependence is established, the addict soon discovers that he suffers withdrawal symptoms without the drug and needs more of the drug to feel good again. Over time, the addict discovers the cost of this dependency—the social, financial, legal, and health consequences of addiction. But he finds himself powerless to deal with the withdrawal symptoms, and, in the words of 12 step support programs, he realizes that his life has become unmanageable.

The shame of discovering you cannot resist the drug, that you are powerless and your life is unmanageable, becomes part of the cycle of addiction. The drug offers relief and a brief sense of grandiosity followed by the despair and shame of withdrawal. Secretly aware of the trap, the addict withdraws into denial (usually with anger at anyone who challenges the denial), and feels more and more isolated and ashamed to acknowledge her powerlessness. This self-isolation has a chance of some relief when the addict arrives at a 12 step meeting, introduces herself tentatively after listening to others in the group do the same, "Hi, I'm Jo, and I'm an alcoholic." The group responds, "Hi, Jo," rather than recoiling in disgust, and the addict's isolation is breached. Some of the shame is relieved by the reconciliation of acceptance by the group of peers. With the support of the group, the addict can discover that powerlessness is not intolerable, and that there are other antidotes for shame besides drugs and denial.

Of course, addiction is a risk that is not limited to those recovering from a loss. Individuals can turn to drugs as solace for the secret shame and depression of adolescence or as a response to a biologically precipitated depression. Or they may be biologically vulnerable to addiction in a culture that uses drugs recreationally. Ten percent of the overall population metabolizes alcohol differently from the other ninety percent.[53] For this ten percent, joining in "normal" young adult drinking behavior can quickly lead to addiction. The percentages are higher for those who experiment recreationally with cocaine, crack, or heroin.

The losses experienced by the families of an addict as the loved one disappears into the addiction are similar to those experienced by the family of someone with a progressive major mental illness. The cycles of powerlessness, shame, and anger evoked for the family members are similar to those of the family of someone disabled by physical illness or injury. Often the anger of family members is aggravated by the assumption that the addiction is a choice rather than an illness. Intimate relationships erode in a losing battle to control the addiction. This is well understood by those who have been through it. Al Anon family support groups are designed to help spouses, partners, parents, and children heal the hurt, shame, and anger that comes as a response to addictive behavior. Often times these patterns are learned by children in a family with an addicted parent. Some teens have found solace in AlaTeen meetings, a smaller number of children benefit from AlaTot programs, and some adults untangle the demons of alcoholic family dynamics by attending Adult Children of Alcoholics meetings.

Shame and Anger in Divorce

Whatever we say about the emotional impact of divorce applies to any relationship in which a significant bond has formed and then is broken. It is a major loss, often experienced as a failure, often as a betrayal. The stages of grief apply to the death of the relationship as surely as they do to the death of a person. But because the other person in this case is not dead, the possibility or necessity of ongoing interaction with the estranged partner is a cruel reminder that triggers the humiliation and anger repeatedly. This makes the acceptance stage difficult to reach. The sense of failure and vulnerability may be hidden by the anger, or the significance of the loss may be denied or rationalized. Nonetheless, these feelings must be experienced and released for a healthy resolution of the grief. Denial and avoidance of the shame and defeat, or suppression of or preoccupation with the anger, require defensive habits of thought and behavior that can trap us behind our emotional bulwarks.

Perhaps, because continuing contact with an estranged partner repeatedly awakens the shame and anger of the grief process, unhealthy grief seems more common in divorce than in death. The partner in the role of betrayer feels accused and reacts with shame and anger. The partner in the role of victim reacts with anger and becomes a persecutor. After a hundred repetitions of this corrosive cycle, negative expectations harden into a distortion of reality, obscuring the possibility of acceptance.

The children of divorce are also subject to the full emotional impact of grief. They have lost their family as they knew it and may feel they have lost access to a relationship with one or both parents, especially if the parents are preoccupied with their own cycles of shame and anger. Children often blame themselves for the divorce, and parents do not understand that the source of this irrational guilt may lie in the shame reaction to the losses of divorce. Or the grief may generate the child's self-directed anger because anger is too dangerous to express toward parents who may leave. Eventually, there is enough anger to spill over onto everyone, including siblings, friends, teachers, and other adults. And there is enough shame to seed a young mind with low self-esteem that shame itself keeps hidden until the behavioral evidence emerges like weeds in a secret garden. There are very few places for children to talk safely about the trials of divorce, very few places for them to hear that their fear, guilt, and anger are normal responses to a major loss. They rarely know that the feelings will pass in time.

Shame and Anger over Aging and Infirmity

Anyone who lives beyond a youthful and vital age experiences some of the losses and indignities of the aging process. Many experience a loss of respect for the value of their work as they reach retirement age. Retirement can bring a crushing sense that your highly valued professional identity has disappeared and rendered you "invisible." Many mourn the loss of beauty and physical agility. Then a series of health challenges and limitations gradually steals comfort, confidence, and independence. A surprising number of older people are able to adjust to these losses gracefully, especially in cultures where their wisdom and status are recognized and their needs supported. But many others find the limitations frustrating or humiliating, especially when cherished favorite activities are no longer possible. Poets from antiquity to modern times bemoan the losses of vitality and comfort that go along with aging, even when the culture compensates the elderly with honor and support.

Shame experienced by the elderly may be seen in many ways, such as the resistance to using a cane or a wheelchair or resistance to considering an assisted living facility. These all represent the loss of mobility or independence or the loss of a familiar and cherished home. Despite vast improvements in hearing aids, many people find them a difficult adjustment and are frequently irritated and embarrassed by the limitations of these devices. In our culture, which places such a high value on youth, aging presents the added humiliation of the loss of status

Shame and Loss

and respect. When one has experienced the peaks of authority and respect in midlife and finds oneself treated with condescension in later years, insult is added to injury and shame can lead to bitterness. An older friend of mine once said, "Sometimes I just want to stand up and shout, 'I used to be somebody!'" Frequently, sincere concern on the part of family members is mistaken for pity, and the resulting bitterness poisons the most supportive of relationships.

Paradoxically, the richer, more active, more creative life can lead to an even longer list of losses to be endured with aging and infirmity. The poet Dylan Thomas urges us to "Rage, rage against the dying of the light."

Shame and Anger in Those Facing Death

The individual with a terminal illness faces more than a single cataclysmic loss. Instead, she endures a series of losses: loss of security, loss of future hopes, loss of physical comfort, mobility, and self-control. There is a loss of dignity that goes along with the loss of independence that is a frequent complaint of terminal patients. These losses, as a result of treatment or the progression of illness, surely evoke the affect of shame as we have come to understand it. But what we usually see most clearly is the anger that may be expressed in many directions–at doctors and nurses, at family and friends, at the healthy, at the body that seems to be betraying us, or at a God who does not seem to respond to our pain and need.

Those who work with and support the dying and the grieving can have a greater tolerance for the normal reactions of anger stemming from this awful helplessness if they have a better understanding of the dynamic emotional impact of loss.

The Rhythm of Resiliency

With such a catalogue of losses to be faced throughout life, and all of them likely to trigger the powerful primary emotions of shame and anger, how can we hope to escape emotional meltdown? Of course, the litany of losses is seldom as densely packed as our summary implies. Time offers room for healing

Chapter Twelve

following a loss, and the dynamic of shame and anger actually works to our advantage in a normal grieving process.

In this dynamic, the pain of grief tends to come in waves. A reminder of the loss evokes sadness and helplessness and we feel beaten down. But the surge of aggression in the shame/anger dynamic picks us up, energizes us, and mobilizes us to get busy and fight the slump, especially if there is work to be done. Then another reminder evokes the pain and powerlessness again, until the automatic anger reaction mobilizes us once more. The waves become less frequent and less intense as time passes and the rhythm of shame and anger massage us into resiliency. This rhythm gives us an opportunity to practice mastering the grief, surviving the loss one wave at a time. If the first wave is too great, shock and denial protect us. Later, anger energizes us. The bargaining phase described by Kubler-Ross seems to reflect this rhythm of defeat and aggression. It is a phase in which we aggressively demand something in return for our loss, and negotiate a gradual letting go. When we are exhausted by the ebb and flow of the process, depression serves to force us to conserve our energy for awhile, until another surge of anger energizes us, or the reconciliation of acceptance frees us to move on in some semblance of balance. In this way, the cycles of shame and anger help us survive overwhelming loss just as they help us survive temporary defeat.

When grief goes awry, it is usually because we are fighting our own normal emotional rhythms. When we deny the pain, hide the shame, or suppress the anger, we block the healing rhythms and find ourselves stalled in a barren landscape, chronically angry or chronically depressed. In most cases, however, the powerful basic emotions emerge in some variation on the rhythm of resiliency so that we are not stalled indefinitely.

Chapter Thirteen
Shame and Society

Shame has been used as a form of overt social control for as long as there have been societies. Those who have violated the social contract in some way have been branded, pilloried in the town square, compelled to wear a scarlet letter, marched before jeering crowds, had their heads shaved, or, more recently, suffered mocking exposure in the press, on TV, and over the internet, all as a way of punishing them with shame in the public forum. The accused often cover their faces, avoid cameras, or retreat behind a bland "no comment" in an attempt to escape the unwanted attention that magnifies their exposure and intensifies their shame. As long as an individual remains thus shamed and stigmatized, he is as cut off from the trust of the society that labels him as if he were in prison.

Many will feel that this is the way it should be, that public shaming is an appropriate and effective method of both punishing offenders and holding up an example of what can happen when society's rules are violated. Others may believe that communities must be very, very sure of the guilt or innocence of the individual before exposing him or her to this cruel, degrading, and humiliating form of punishment. Still others may want these shaming sanctions eliminated unless there are clear methods for societal reconciliation available to bring the persons being vilified back into the fold. Whatever moral stance we may bring to this issue personally, there is no doubt that many feel our society has moved too far into the use of public vilification for offenses that may be intrinsic to individual human beings, may never have occurred at all, or may have been blown out of all proportion in the need to fill the 24 hour news cycle.

While the major purpose of this book is to explore the ways in which the emotions of shame and anger and our difficulties with criticism impact our personal lives, we cannot ignore the fact that the use of shame in the context of our larger society impacts us as well. We find our identities and play our roles in the numerous communities in which we live—our neighborhoods, towns, states, and nations—but also in our race, gender, ethnicity, physical and mental ability, and socio-economic group. We participate in society as part of the great public mass that assigns or accepts the shaming of segments of our population. We are also members of groups that are, or could be, shamed by others.

Of course, whole libraries have been written on subjects such as race and gender inequality and the resulting shame felt by those who are discriminated against and thus made to feel unworthy. Many people trace the most deeply shameful feelings of their lives to natural, inherent factors over which they have no control and for which they, objectively, should feel no shame at all. Attributes such as skin color, sexual orientation, learning disabilities, physical handicaps, less than perfectly formed bodies or faces, intellectual limitations, and myriad other characteristics are deemed by particular societies to be less than acceptable. Once again, the fear of the different, the "other," the "not like us"—this time vastly magnified on a societal scale—

carries us to emotions of distain and disrespect that we should seek to overcome.

The mentality and behavior dictated by conformity to the mass society can only change when enough individuals find reason to resist the temptation to go along with excessive shaming. A greater understanding of the role that shame plays in society may help us play our roles as members of that society more thoughtfully. If we can each learn that shame and anger are part of our basic emotional equipment of powerful primitive affects and also learn how to manage these emotions so that they do not misguide us so often, we will be better able to negotiate both intimate personal relationships and public discourse. Because the subject is so vast, we will focus on several modern phenomena to make a few important points.

Shame and Reconciliation in Societies

In the bosom of the family, a child should be able to make mistakes, accept some censure or punishment, and be reconciled back into full participation in family life. This push and pull of shame and reconciliation is a powerful incentive to learn and comply with the social norms taught in the family. Some small societies ritualize reconciliation as elaborately as most ritualize shame and punishment. The following ritual is described in Jack Kornfield's book, The Art of Forgiveness, Loving-kindness, and Peace.

"In the Babemba tribe of South Africa, when a person acts irresponsibly or unjustly, he is placed in the center of the village, alone and unfettered. All work ceases, and every man, woman, and child in the village gathers in a large circle around the accused individual. Then each person in the tribe speaks to the accused, one at a time, each recalling the good things the person in the center of the circle has done in his lifetime. Every incident, every experience that can be recalled with any detail and accuracy, is recounted. All his positive attributes, good deeds, strengths, and kindnesses are recited carefully and at length. This tribal ceremony often lasts for several days. At the end, the tribal circle is broken, a joyous celebration takes place, and the person is symbolically and literally welcomed back into the tribe."[54]

In this example, the shame is implied by the fact that an enormous effort is made by the entire community to reconcile the offender to society. The offense and the shame are made more obvious to the offender by the extreme emphasis on past positive qualities and strengths and the community's focus on forgiveness.

In an intimate social group, such as a family, tribe, or small village, an individual's offenses and his shame are more easily known to others in the group. An individual under the influence of the affect of shame seeks to withdraw or become invisible until his membership status is reestablished. But if the social group is small enough, and if it is essential to one's survival, withdrawal is not an option. Shame is intensified when the shamed individual is the focus of attention. If there is no viable option to further shaming and ostracism, the desire for reconciliation will be overwhelming.

Hiding in a Large Social Environment

Few of us live in villages anymore. In our large and open society, individuals can maintain a much higher degree of anonymity than in former times, withdrawing or disappearing into a mass of urban humanity. Uncounted dysfunctional individuals and families hide beneath a veil of anonymity and seek to avoid the attention of those around them which would intensify the internal experience of shame as well as the exposure and the risk of ostracism. But if they maintain anonymity, they also forgo the possibility of reconciliation and full membership in a basic group such as a family or neighborhood. Very few individuals are content in this socially isolated state of being. We are hardwired to be safer and happier as members of social groups. So an individual who escapes shame by isolation is likely to become unhappy and angry—and the anger can be directed at the self or the society from which he is an outcast, or at both. Angry antisocial behavior can further deepen the isolation and erode the possibility of reconciliation. The individual then no longer hopes to belong but seeks only to exercise and experience power, substituting the safety of power for the safety of belonging.

Some will satisfy the need for belonging by joining subgroups with an antisocial focus, such as a gang or cult. Part of the power of these groups is the belief of many members that they have nowhere else to belong. If they do not fit in this group, they are doomed to isolation. If the gang or cult requires more and more extreme evidence of compliance with group mores as the cost of belonging, the members become even more trapped in their dilemma.

Shame and Discrimination in the Context of Society

Members of a minority group, or even members of a powerless majority, when subjected to prolonged and consistent shaming, can lose the hope of belonging. When individuals are subjected to too much shame without hope of reconciliation, they can eventually become so enraged and hopeless that the possibility of reconciliation becomes meaningless. They no longer seek to belong and are chronically angry. They can turn anger inward and become depressed and defeated or they can turn to a culture of anger and violence directed at others. Young unemployed men, ashamed of their status, are difficult to motivate and may express their frustration in antisocial behaviors.

Groups of adolescents who are consistently excluded and humiliated by the dominant popular group can turn to violence as an outlet for the anger and a way to end the humiliation. Such episodes of violence in high schools and middle schools in this country have often been attributed to unstable families, the availability of guns, violence in the media, and other societal factors, but the emotional drivers for such extreme actions almost certainly have their primary roots in shame and rage generated by social discrimination and isolation. The recent release of research into the mindset of the young people who carried out the Columbine massacre indicates that they were enraged by ostracism, isolation, and shaming by popular peers in their school.

When one subset of the population is consistently excluded and humiliated by a dominant group through racial, religious, or sexual discrimination, the dynamics of shame and anger become cast in social group behavior that replicate the personal and individual shame events thousands of times over. Specific historical events, such as lost battles or atrocities committed by one group upon another, take on special significance symbolic of the humiliation and keep the memory of shame and hatred alive until it becomes the fabric of a feud that endures for generation after generation. The "troubles" between Protestants and Catholics in Northern Ireland, the battles between Sunni and Shia in the Middle East, and violence between Christians, Muslims, and Jews throughout the last two thousand years are all examples of longstanding feuds in which anniversaries of past defeats become the occasion for new outbreaks of retribution. Defusing such deeply rooted hatreds is extremely difficult because it is all but impossible to halt the ongoing hurts and insults that reopen old wounds, and it is very easy to evoke powerful cultural memories of past injustice.

The efforts of Bishop Desmond Tutu and the Truth and Reconciliation Commission in South Africa are a determined plan to balance justice and forgiveness to heal the wounds of apartheid. Individuals confessing their discriminatory and harmful behavior are accepting shame for their actions by virtue of the act of confession. In the context of the forum for truth and reconciliation, they face the relatives and friends of those whom they have harmed. This is a context that offers reconciliation that helps release the anger and break the cycle of retribution. Powerful as these rituals are, we can expect that the job of nurturing forgiveness and equality will require many generations to complete.

Shame and Alienation

Whenever a society depends on shame and harsh judgment as emotional instruments of social control without the balancing mechanisms of forgiveness and reconciliation, there will be long term consequences. In some rigidly moralistic groups, the threat of public censure is the primary mechanism for maintaining the social norms of the society. But as more and more members of society are judged, ostracized, and shamed without possibility of reconciliation, there is a growing subculture of alienated and angry members with the potential to defy the dominant group. Feelings of inferiority may hold the powerless minority class of the condemned back from defiant action for some time, but anger continues to build until something sparks a revolution.

At the same time, members of the dominant group may suffer from fear that they, too, may be judged and cast out, or they may become increasingly uncomfortable with the tensions between the two groups. In racial reconciliation encounter groups, where individuals from minorities and majorities meet together to talk truthfully about their feelings, open expression of fear, anger, shame, and guilt from both sides of the cultural divide can lead to a striking release of tension followed by mutual respect and reconciliation.

Shaming Penal Systems

When the legal and penal systems for punishing offenders rely on humiliating punishment and continued exposure to social condemnation without support for rehabilitation, we can expect a high rate of recidivism. Offenders who are already outcast and angry are further isolated by incarceration from opportunities for participation in normal society. They are accepted only by a peer group of fellow offenders in the outcast population. When efforts at rehabilitation and careful transition back to normal society are minimal, the offender sees no hope of reconciliation, identifies primarily with the antisocial population of offenders, and continues to act out of humiliation and anger, resulting in more antisocial behavior. Strong families are sometimes able to welcome an individual back into his home after incarceration, and through balancing acceptance with expectations of socially appropriate behavior, help heal the wounds of shame and anger. Rehabilitation services and prison ministries can sometimes offer offenders opportunities for relationships with others outside the outcast world that affirm his value in the larger society and open doors to reconciliation. Yet the stigma of social ostracism is still difficult to overcome and the private feelings of shame and anger can sabotage even sincere efforts at rehabilitation.

Shame and Celebrity

On the opposite end of the social spectrum from those discriminated against and those incarcerated, we have people who appear to have grabbed the golden apple of life but are also uniquely vulnerable to shaming by society. In a civilization where the overwhelming majority of individuals are unknown to one another, a few become celebrities. We tend to focus our media attention on various stars, athletes, leaders, and heroes, but also on some who become notorious because of crime or scandal, or by pure accident. Celebrity is a fickle phenomenon. Some crave and seek the attention and recognition that celebrity brings, only to find themselves hounded by paparazzi, open to outrageous rumor mongering in the tabloids, or stalked by some of their most ardent fans (short for fanatics). We tend to hold our celebrities (with the exception of the notorious ones) to high standards as role models for our children. We may assign hero status to a ball player with superior talent and skills and expect him to live by behavioral standards we do not really expect of ourselves or other people. When he does not meet those expectations, even if he is not breaking a law or written rule, he may be subjected to severe criticism in the public forum.

Young Olympic athletes who often have sacrificed years of normal youthful activity to the rigors of training are not only expected to excel at their sport under intense competitive pressure and scrutiny, but also expected to demonstrate poise, maturity, and humility beyond their years along with confidence and determination. When they do not live up to these unrealistic and sometimes contradictory expectations, we are disappointed in them. However tactfully this disappointment is expressed by columnist or commentator, the young celebrity knows her failure is magnified in a global media lens.

Shame and Society

We also expect the leaders we elect to know every aspect of the complex world they are leading, to please everyone while telling the truth at all times, to work long hours and then raise money for campaigning on the side, to create clear solutions for complex problems, and to live at all times by a standard of behavior most of us would not apply to ourselves. When our leaders fail to meet these high standards, they become targets for their opponents and for the media.

Shaming our celebrities may function in a way that diverts us from awareness of our own failings. By distancing ourselves from our celebrities, placing them on a pedestal, we may also generate envy for the attention they receive—envy that finds some satisfaction in the celebrity's downfall, even while we decry it.

Shame and the Polarization of Political Debate

For similar reasons, attack ads have become ubiquitous in the landscape of 21st Century American political campaigns and are now spreading around the world. Typically these ads seek to exaggerate some aspect of the opponent's position on an issue or some aspect of his character to a point where it is viewed as shameful or hateful. Such vividly crafted attacks can create issue-specific identities that isolate and demonize candidates who share many values with their opponents but differ in their opinions on one issue. The result of competing attack ad campaigns is that public respect for both opponents is damaged and such a high degree of public anger is aroused that it is difficult for the candidate who wins to lead effectively.

Talk show hosts who entertain their listeners by shaming callers with differing opinions rather than trying to conduct a constructive dialogue, contribute to a culture of shame and anger in the same way that school yard bullies entertain their audiences by making fun of another child.

Alternatives for an Emotionally Intelligent Society

We are vulnerable to emotional manipulation because of our need to escape emotions we do not understand and that therefore operate without our full awareness. When we do not understand our feelings of powerlessness, shame, and anger in response to complex problems in our own lives or in the larger world, we are not aware of the possibility of healthy relief from these feelings. When someone offers us a chance to focus blame on somebody else, diverting attention from our own shame and engaging our anger, we find it hard to resist. We are off balance in our surrender posture and easily influenced by emotional arguments. There is evidence that the emotions of fear and anger are more contagious and more easily manipulated in the context of the mass or mob.

There is no better example of the use of mass shaming in the 20th Century than the Cultural Revolution in the People's Republic of China between 1966 and 1976. During this period, millions of people were motivated by fear and propaganda to demonize their neighbors. Thousands were subjected to public shaming events in which they were forced into postures of submission for hours in front of screaming crowds until they "criticized" themselves in public confession. Family ties were decimated by communal living and youth and students were set against elders. Fear and shaming were used as tools for undermining traditional family and social allegiances and were most effectively demonstrated in mass meetings where fear of being targeted could be magnified as a powerful incentive for cooperation rather than resistance.

In order to be able to resist the primal response of fear, shame, and anger evoked in stressful social situations, we need a solid grounding in emotional intelligence. We need to understand the basic equipment of our powerful primitive emotions, how they can misguide us, and then to learn a new way of managing these emotions. Such learning does not normally take place on a societal level any more than learning language or music skills. Although a society may share a common language or value musical skill, the basics are learned at the family or neighborhood level through daily interactions and practice.

The process of learning and practicing emotional intelligence skills for quieting shame and anger and cultivating opportunities for reconciliation is more appropriate and practicable at the family or village level, where rituals like those of the Babemba tribe can include all the members of the group. Healthy trust forged in family and village intimacy serves as a buffer against some of the threats and dangers of larger societal pressures. Even in the cauldron of the Cultural Revolution, strong family ties such as those described in Jung Chang's memoir, The Wild Swans, provided a powerful resource for resilience.[55]

The skills for taming shame and anger rather than simply suppressing them are subtle, require continuing support and practice, and are constantly subject to erosion by primal instincts and larger societal pressures. A growing awareness of the importance of emotional intelligence is leading to the development of training programs that can be offered to families or used in small classes in schools. Promoting Alternative Thinking Strategies (PATHS)[56] is one such program. PATHS is used in over a hundred school districts in the United States and shown to be effective in reducing aggression and violence and promoting cooperation in the classroom.[57] Most of the emotional awareness and emotional management skills taught in this program can be learned and taught by parents at the family level.

In A World Waiting to be Born, Scott Peck describes a process that can be practiced by a work group or team, such as a board of directors or an ongoing committee.[58] In this process, time and care are devoted to establishing intimacy and trust among a group of strangers brought together for a common goal so that the fear of shame and angry competition do not undermine creativity and cooperative support within the group. Peck stresses the primacy of maintaining this trust and intimacy through reparative attention to any erosion of trust.

Establishing this kind of intimacy and trust seems to work best in small groups approximately the size of an extended family group. Therapy groups are often limited to eight to ten members so that the trust and intimacy necessary for sharing sensitive issues is not undermined by the fear of exposure in a much larger group. It is not likely that an entire society would quickly adopt a culture of trust and reconciliation, but it may be possible to establish a culture of intimacy and trust in enough small groups that the values, skills, and rituals of reconciliation eventually become common in more and more communities and then, finally, in larger societies.

Beyond the home, the classroom, and the work team lie the larger communities of our lives – churches and other religious institutions, neighborhood groups of all types, clubs and fraternal organizations, political, professional, and business associations, and many others. Community institutions can be powerful forces for sharing honest and open communication on issues that trigger shame and anger, or they can move in the opposite direction and become dangerous weapons of scapegoating and rage. The "cultures" of such organizations are powerful tools for moving the individual members and the larger society forward or backward on the spectrum of emotional intelligence. As individual members of these groups, we have a positive responsibility to move such cultures toward honesty and openness and away from shaming behaviors that inevitably lead to anger and even violence.

Large groups of people, however, are easily swayed by those who deplore, who disparage, who "view with alarm." As a friend of mine said, "It's easy to get a quorum on what's wrong with the other guy." So it is not easy to exercise positive influence on the culture of large groups against a tide of fear, shame, and anger. But with a clear plan and disciplined follow through, it is possible.

As we discussed above, it is more natural and feasible to establish trust and intimacy among members of a small group and it is an increasingly common practice within organizations to break into small discussion groups when difficult subjects must be discussed or decisions made. When trust is established in a small group, this group provides enough protection to its members to allow them to take risks in larger gatherings.

Community organizers for the Industrial Areas Foundation, trained in the grass roots social organizing principles developed by Saul Alinsky, who pioneered community strategies for social change, routinely begin their work on social issues in a diverse urban community by insisting that members of the community meet and get to know one another personally. They are encouraged to develop trust through one-on-one meetings and small groups before issues such as school systems or housing improvements are ever discussed. These organizers know that the grass roots alliances they hope to forge will break down in competition over leadership and suspicion of the stranger unless trust can be built as a first order of business. Community leaders, often clergymen and women who already have the trust of their own congregations, are enlisted to encourage their members to take the chance to meet and get to know others outside of their own circles. Trust, based on personal connections built in one-on-one conversations and shared meals, is extended to the larger body of the organization, and this can enable the group to weather the tensions that will emerge in pursuit of a common mission that can only be accomplished through the political power of a large group.

We have the motivation, the ability, and the opportunity to promote emotional intelligence skills that will enable us to resist fear, shame, and anger. Our next goal must be to let as many people as possible know about these skills. If we exemplify them in our own lives, and let others know how important they are, how to acquire them, and how to teach them to our children, we can begin to create a society where fear, shame, and anger do not overwhelm emotional intelligence and civil discourse – building it one family, classroom, or community at a time. Cultural evolution can happen much more quickly than biological evolution. We do not have to wait for our basic emotional equipment to evolve. We can begin to apply skills for emotional intelligence and managing our powerful emotions now.

In the meantime, there are several steps we can take to assure that, as individual citizens of our individual societies, we are less likely to be manipulated by the forces of shame and anger in their societal manifestations.

∞ We can listen to the vibrations of our own internal shame and anger meters to determine if we are being driven to emotions of hate and fear of specific groups by tactics of guilt by association—the accusation that "they" are the source of our pain / poverty / danger / threat / inconvenience.

∞ We can refuse to listen to demagogic rants in the media and among our friends against groups or individuals.

∞ We can refuse to vote for or support politicians or civic leaders who demonize their opponents by unproven accusations and inflammatory rhetoric.

∞ We can try to influence the organizations and communities of which we are a part to follow a path of inclusion, honesty, and support for positive, rather than negative, goals and methods of operation.

∞ We can seek to judge, because as adults we must make judgments, on the basis of information and not accusation.

∞ We can always ask, "Are those who are placed outside the pale of societal tolerance and acceptance, for whatever reason, offered a way back into the fold in my community?"

Chapter Fourteen
Shame and Spirituality

One cannot read for very long in search of answers to the questions of human pain and suffering without encountering the vast literature of religion and spirituality. The topics of shame and anger crop up regularly in religious texts. Although much that has been written on the spiritual realm deals with a very different set of concepts than those of brain function and evolutionary psychology, it is intriguing to notice how much common ground exists between the two areas. This is especially evident when we look at the activities and expectations in what is usually called "spiritual practice."

Some readers will associate religious institutions and teachings with the social enforcement of moral codes, enforcement that has frequently been accomplished with liberal doses of shame. Religious institutions and rituals have often become part of the fabric of social control, reinforcing conformity with societal values and the existing power structure. Jared Diamond suggests that the power hierarchies of many societies seek to co-opt religious institutions so that they do not compete with the state for the loyalty of the people.[59] Thus intense shaming and cruel punishment have sometimes been associated with religious institutions that are allied with the state. Mutilation and human sacrifice sanctioned by primitive religious ritual, the tortures of the Spanish Inquisition, "shunning" by a closed religious community, and the threat of excommunication are all examples of situations in which religion has been part of the power structure of a society.

To the extent that it is possible to differentiate spiritual practice from institutional religion, I would like to do so here. The spiritual practices to which I refer are means by which individuals seek meaning and value in the experience of a life that inevitably also involves pain, loss, and danger. They are often found in scriptures and teachings that are the foundations of institutional religion, but they can also be read and understood independently of the religious institutions associated with them.

Shame and the Problem of Good and Evil

The human experience of shame in defeat contrasted with the sense of power and glory that comes from being allied with an almighty spiritual Lord is a recurring theme in Hebrew and Islamic scriptures as well as many other ancient texts. The first mention of shame in the Bible, however, is the shame of Adam and Eve in their nakedness. They have been discovered, or exposed, if you will, in their ambition to become like God, having the power to judge good and evil. Their consequent expulsion from paradise can be read as a mythic event that points to a fact of life that philosophers, spiritual leaders, and psychologists ever since have explored in great depth. The fact of life I refer to is that a great deal of human suffering can be directly attributed to man's ability, and seeming compulsion, to distinguish good from evil, and to acquire the good and avoid the evil.

Shame and Spirituality

A great deal of thought has gone into attempts to define good and evil, or right and wrong, by reference to logic or "natural" and universal moral perceptions. But even when there is agreement about the definitions, we seem woefully unable to achieve a lasting state in which good and right consistently prevail and bad or wrong are eliminated.

From the point of view of evolutionary psychology, we might say that the mythic event described in the story of Adam and Eve points to the moment in evolutionary time when humans began to use their brains to anticipate problems and try to solve or avoid them—to gain the good and avoid the bad. The ability to do this has led to the survival of the better planners and, through them, the development of civilization. The consequences of this ability, however, are subtle but powerful. In order to avoid the bad or wrong path consistently, you have to think about it. You have to distinguish between some future imagined event you consider good, and a future event you consider bad. In other words, you have to judge.

Making the distinction between eating and being eaten in terms of good or bad is a no-brainer. Similar distinctions between being safe or sorry in many respects are natural and unavoidable. But we make many other distinctions that are not necessary for survival because of our highly developed ability to judge. Our big brains are capable of imagining many alternative futures, some of which are not only safer than others, but also more comfortable or more pleasant. The act of making such choices tends to be self-reinforcing, like the behavior of the experimental laboratory rat whose brain is stimulated in the pleasure center every time he presses a lever in his cage. The confidence that we can control the future feels good. Judging and choosing gives us hope. Hope feels good. And so does the judging and choosing that give us hope if we are relatively successful in achieving our choices. Loss of hope and loss of a sense of control, even if the control was an illusion, feels bad. It is a fate we try to avoid. So the mental behavior of judging and choosing in order to maintain our sense of control tends to become compulsive.

Chapter Fourteen

Over the ages, the survival advantage humans acquired by making rapid judgments has evolved into a compulsion to distinguish preferences, to judge some circumstances, events, or people as good and others as bad, even when they are not clearly associated with a survival advantage. We speculated in Chapter 2 as to how this compulsion for judging could have evolved. The ability to judge has been passed down through countless generations, honed and shaped through family and tribal tradition so that we can learn to label a person or situation that is merely different as being dangerous or undesirable. From this ability, turned compulsion, come the many shaming evils of prejudice and intolerance that plague our relationships with one another and the societies in which we live today.

There is a second subtle consequence of the human ability to judge between good and bad. In order to avoid the bad, after identifying it in your mind, you have to think about it some more. You have to anticipate the undesirable event and its potentially negative ramifications in order to figure out how to avoid it. In other words, you have to worry. Because evolution rewards those able to anticipate and avoid certain bad things like attack by predators or defeat by one's enemies, humans have evolved an extensive capacity for worrying about dangers, risks, and problems in the future. Yet all our planning, worrying, and striving for control consistently fail to secure the good for very long. On the contrary, worrying tends to drain our energy. Because there is no end to possible future threats about which we can worry, this compulsion will inevitably leave us defeated, shamed, and angry.

Shame and the Need for Power and Control

Those who amass wealth and power in order to secure their own "good" tend to trample the rights and welfare of others in the process. This can be true of groups as well as individuals, even when the members of the powerful group are unaware that the rights and welfare of other groups are being trampled. The purchasers of discounted diamonds are generally unaware that the stones are exported by ruthless mercenaries in Africa who obtain them though violence and use the profits to support more violence. The purchase supports the violence regardless of the purchasers' ignorance. Those of us who enjoy big cars and relatively low gas prices in the U.S. may be carelessly trampling on the welfare of others in less affluent lands because they are less able to protect themselves from the consequences of poor air quality and global warming.

Power is not a perfect shield, however. Mighty individuals can be brought low in dramatic reversals of fortune. Often they are betrayed by those closest to them when their wealth and power are coveted as the guarantee of personal safety and wellbeing. Roman emperors lived in fear of assassination by family members or their own guards. And even when the mighty are able to hold onto power to the end, they must ultimately face death, perhaps passing through the indignities of illness and aging on the way. In the world of power, like the world of survival, defeat evokes shame and rage. The defeated must bow their heads in submission and shame to the newly powerful and victorious. As soon as the balance of power shifts, the name of the formerly godlike ruler is cursed and defaced. His gold packed tomb is robbed and defiled, and his monuments are toppled.

Poets and historians capture the futility of the quest for control among even the most glorious and powerful. Shelley's classic poem, *Ozymandius*, comes to mind.

> I met a traveler from an antique land
> Who said: "Two vast and trunkless legs of stone
> Stand in the desert... Near them, on the sand,
> Half sunk, a shattered visage lies, whose frown,
> And wrinkled lip, and sneer of cold command,
> Tell that its sculptor well those passions read
> Which yet survive, stamped on these lifeless things,
> The hand that mocked them and the heart that fed;
> And on the pedestal these words appear:
> 'My name is Ozymandius, King of Kings:
> Look on my works, ye Mighty, and despair!'
> Nothing beside remains. Round the decay

Chapter Fourteen

Of that colossal wreck, boundless and bare
The lone and level sands stretch far away."

Shame and anger and obsession with power and control have been acted out in ever larger dramas on the stage of human history for thousands of years.

∞ The war between Greeks and Trojans recorded in Homer's Iliad is an epic saga of egos struggling with shame and rage that constantly threaten to undermine ideals of courage and nobility. When the two armies are exhausted, they agree to let their two champions, Hector and Achilles, fight to the death with the outcome of their duel determining the outcome of the war. Achilles kills Hector, but in an unnecessary show of hubris, drags his body around the city behind his chariot. Troy is humiliated by this blatant disrespect for their hero. The usually passive Paris is so enraged that he shoots an arrow into Achilles' heel, killing him and infuriating the Greeks, and the battle is on again full bore.

∞ The German nation, humiliated after World War I by the terms of the Treaty of Versailles and taxed into economic depression by required reparations, found this shame untenable and sought release in the power and pride of nationalism that led to World War II twenty years later. The restoration of German society and economic stability through the Marshall Plan helped avert a recurrence of this pattern following WWII.

∞ From the occupation of Israel by Roman legions in the First Century to the occupation of Palestinian territories by Israel in the 21st century, shamed citizens of occupied countries have been spurred to fierce, often suicidal, resistance by their feelings of helplessness and shame.

∞ The war that began in 2003 in Iraq bogged down in a guerilla insurgency that can be linked to the rage response to a humiliating military occupation. "There is strong evidence, based on a review of thousands of

Shame and Spirituality

military documents and hundreds of interviews with military personnel, that the U.S. approach to pacifying Iraq helped spur the insurgency and made it bigger and stronger than it might have been. ... Few U.S. soldiers seemed to understand the centrality of Iraqi pride and the humiliation Iraqi men felt in being overseen by this Western army."[60]

At some point in the evolution of civilization, long before any of the examples listed above, humans obtained enough security to recognize the down side of our proficiency at worrying and our compulsion to judge and control. Historians of religion refer to the Axial Age, from 800-600 BC, when people began to reflect on the meaning of life beyond survival, security, and comfort. Prior to the Axial Age, primitive tribal religions sought to influence the mysterious powers of nature to the advantage of the tribe by sacrifice and other practices intended to win the support of a god or spirit. During the Axial Age a new prosperity led to the rise of a merchant class in developed civilizations and the social phenomena of inequality and exploitation became more apparent. Ideologies that emphasized the values of justice and mercy began to emerge, became popular, then prominent, as a reaction to the concentration of wealth and power that expanded commercial activity brought in its wake. The major religions in the world today took root in these ideologies. Peace and compassion, in both social and psychological contexts, became as important as power.[61]

Surrender Without Shame

One of the common elements in these religions or spiritual movements was that surrender to ultimate reality or to a supreme and merciful deity need not be shameful. The individual who submits to "the will of God" or who obeys, even while protesting God's distance (as did several of the Hebrew prophets), is able to accept life as a gift with both the joy and the suffering inherent in the experience of it. In more modern or secular terms, one who accepts the realities of the human condition can find a sense of peace in his existence that is not available to those who struggle for control.

A contemporary interpretation of the *Rule of St. Benedict*, a set of guidelines for living well in community, stresses this:

> "Live this life and do whatever is done in a spirit of
>   Thanksgiving.
> Abandon attempts to achieve security, they are futile,
> Give up the search for wealth, it is demeaning,
> Quit the search for salvation, it is selfish,
> And come to comfortable rest in the certainty that those
>   who participate in this life with an attitude of
>   Thanksgiving will receive its full promise." [62]

The individual who accepts reality without trying to manipulate it to his own advantage is uplifted rather than bowed down in defeat. Some who are facing certain death are able to find peace, a transcendent freedom from worry, anger, or shame. In Buddhist thought this individual is freed from the futile illusion that he can control or change reality and becomes "enlightened." Surrender, in this context, is not a shameful defeat, but a wise and freeing acceptance of ultimate reality, a willing alliance with the incomprehensible source of existence. Only those who persist in struggling to achieve control for themselves or on their own terms are thwarted and end feeling defeated, helpless, and shamed. In Buddhist terms, the one who continues to try to control reality is caught up in the inexorable cycle of suffering. The spiritual solution then is surrender without shame and acceptance of what we cannot change.

Focus on Now versus Future or Past

The spiritual practices recommended to help people achieve this surrender without shame often involve a focus on the present rather than the future or past. In psychological terms, excessive focus on concerns about the past or future tend to generate shame or anxiety. Though we can plan and prepare for the future to some extent, there are always variables beyond our control. Compulsive efforts to eliminate uncertainty in all these

Shame and Spirituality

variables inevitably bring us face to face with our own helplessness, a shaming experience. Focus on regrets about the past can easily slip from the review of lessons learned into a futile desire to relive and change the past. Naturally, this proves to be impossible. Though we can decide to reinterpret the past to some psychological advantage, to make ourselves more comfortable, or change a past mistake into a commitment to change, continued review of dissatisfaction with past action simply deepens the sense of failure and helplessness and therefore intensifies shame and anger. When an individual person is caught up in such a counterproductive review of the past, he is generating the foundations for depression. When tribes, nations or cultures engage in this process, they give birth to feuds that can last a thousand years. Serbians have been celebrating victory over Albanians with self-satisfying contempt for their enemies for over 600 years. Hutu harbored hatred for their brother Tutsi for one hundred years before breaking out in murderous violence. Groups that ritually review the defeats of the past fuel shame and anger and a hunger for revenge.

Spiritual advisors often encourage disciples to let go of the past, spend little time contemplating the future, and stay awake in the present. The psychological benefit of following this advice, practicing a focus on the present, is to interrupt the compulsive game of reviewing past mistakes and planning anxiously for the future. Many practitioners of such present-centered spiritual disciplines report that interrupting their usual mode of anxious planning and regretful remembering leads to a blissful state, a peaceful acceptance of the moment—even when the moment contains pain or distress we might otherwise compulsively seek to avoid.

Therapy for patients in chronic pain often includes a recognition that the suffering is magnified by both the review of remembered pain and the fear of anticipated pain. Their lives are constricted by the compulsion to avoid expected repetition of remembered pain. Considerable relief can be achieved through techniques designed to help patients deal with the pain in the present moment only and resist devoting attention to pain avoidance. Massage therapists will encourage their clients to breathe into the pain of a knotted muscle and release the tension that the individual is holding onto unconsciously. Most attempts to contain or avoid pain are self-defeating.

Compassion versus Competition

Another theme found in most spiritual practices is the exercise of compassion for others. The ability to empathize with the suffering of others, to care deeply about their pain or misfortune, is a quality attributed to spiritual leaders, saints, sages, and even to the images of God in many traditions.

From a psychological point of view, the exercise of compassion—like the focus on the present moment—works to interrupt anxious, self-centered worrying or shameful, self-centered regret, because compassion is "other" centered. The brain cannot focus on too many things at the same time, and self-concern usually trumps everything else. When we are preoccupied with worry or shame, we tend to withdraw into our own world, the world dominated by our pain. But when compassionate focus is exercised with sufficient intensity, when you are highly focused on the needs or welfare of another, your attention to your own pain is interrupted. Many parents and caretakers can remember times when their awareness of their own discomfort or danger vanished in the face of their child's need, distress, or danger.

The experience of compassion seems to stand in opposition to the drive to compete and win that favors survival and evolutionary advance. Nature often seems to favor the most ruthless and efficient predators. But mathematical theories of the dynamics involved in the evolution of groups have shown compassion to be a valuable element in the survival of the group.[63] Higher primates, including humans, with the ability to protect their young and sacrifice for the welfare of the family or social group have an advantage over species for whom individual competition for resources is the unwavering rule. So we appear to be hardwired with the capacity for compassion, but this wiring is most evident in the protection of the young or the immediate family. The practice of generalizing compassion for others beyond our circle of family and friends can help develop compassion into a mental focus that takes precedence over other default thoughts and feelings. We have already discussed how the practice of worrying can lead to development of anxiety disorders and other self-reinforcing mental habits. Conversely, the practice of compassion can lead to a state of peaceful calm and hope even in the midst of great trials. This has been demonstrated by great souls in contemporary times, individuals such as Mahatma Gandhi, the Dalai Lama, Thich Nhat Hahn, and Thomas Merton.

One fascinating finding of recent brain research is that the area of the brain stimulated by compassionate focus is the same area associated with deep contentment or calm joy—the left prefrontal lobe of the cerebral cortex. This is distinct from the area of the brain stimulated by worry, fear, or anger—the emergency survival processing center in the right prefrontal lobe. Thus the statement of the Dalai Lama to the effect that "the first beneficiary of the practice of compassionate meditation is the practitioner himself," appears to be confirmed by modern scientific research. The person absorbed in compassionate concern for the welfare of others is thereby freed from anxious self-concern and experiences a sense of peace that can modulate self-centered anxiety through the concern for another person.

Forgiveness versus Vengeance

One of the greatest themes and tensions in all religious literature and teaching is the question of vengeance versus forgiveness. In ancient Hebrew scriptures, vengeance against their enemies is promised to the chosen people. The vengeance will be provided by God because of their loyalty and because he has chosen to shield them with his favor. But vengeance is not to be taken by individuals. It is constrained by deference to sacred law or obedience to God who, alone, has the right to sit in judgment. Even when men are encouraged to execute judgments against other men with ruthless acts of vengeance, it is usually clear that they are acting on behalf of God, the higher judge—not taking vengeance themselves or as their own right. Men are encouraged to treat one another justly, with humility and mercy, forgiving debts and limiting revenge to "an eye for an eye." In the later Hebrew scriptures and the Christian scriptures, mercy, forgiveness, humility, and compassion are emphasized, consistent with the ideologies that evolved in the Axial Age. Such compassion is also taught in all of the other great religions of the world.

From a psychological point of view, when an individual, a tribe, or a nation is defeated, wronged, and humiliated, they are compelled to reduce the shame evoked by the memory of that humiliation or defeat. The desire to balance the scales through counter attack or revenge can be imagined, discussed, planned, and passed on through generations of oral and written history, so that the humiliation and desire for vengeance is kept alive. Every time a memory is revisited, it is more deeply memorized. Neurologists explain this by saying that "neurons that fire together, wire together." The processes of memory are advanced by practice and repetition. Reviewing a grudge keeps it strong.

The affective (feeling) component of the burden of an angry memory is the biochemical assault, the flood of aggressive hormones, triggered by the affect of anger associated with the memory. This powerful emotional charge further reinforces the memory and deepens the association of anger and the memory. After a few dozen repetitions, it becomes very difficult to think of the incident or the persons involved without an angry emotional response. The powerful emotions of fear, shame, and anger are like alarm bells or red flares sending us to battle stations and reinforcing our identity with the fear-focused, problem-solving ego. The more often our emotional brains become highly aroused, the more sensitive we are to any threat. The more we tend to scan the past and future for evidence of danger, the more we fear letting go of control.

In addition to the fact that such vengeful anger tends to compel us to rash and sometimes dangerous acts, the emotional state itself is physically stressful, and anyone who lives with hatred and frequent flares of anger will suffer the exhausting strain of chronic stress. Vengeance, the angry memory, has been compared to a rusty sword in your heart that only you can remove.

From an evolutionary point of view, this ability and compulsion to remember pain and defeat helps us to avoid some practical problems in living. Remembering a danger or a mistake allows us to plan to avoid it in the future. But when it becomes a rusty sword in the heart, it creates a new danger, a health risk to individuals and societies alike, one that can only be healed by letting go of the fantasy of revenge and opening up to forgiveness.

The spiritual solution to the debilitating hope for revenge is forgiveness, one of the means by which we let go of regrets and disappointments and refocus on the gifts of the present. I believe it was Landrum Bolling, noted educator and advocate for peace in the Middle East, who coined the phrase, "Forgiveness means giving up all hope of a better past." This profound quip points to the absurdity of hoping for the impossible and can help free us from the regret and resentment associated with a painful history.

Forgiveness offers a way out of the trap of vengeance, but it is far from intuitive. Learning to love one's enemies is one of life's most difficult emotional and spiritual challenges. Enlightenment, forgiveness, and being "born again" are almost always associated with "ego death"—or waking up from the "dream of ego" in which we believe that we must and can control our own fate by remembering the past, anticipating the future, and acting to shape it. The ego, that part of us that thrives on control, fights to keep control. As a consequence, relinquishing the "hope" of revenge and control is never easy.

Some spiritual disciplines teach that it requires the courage of a warrior to be willing to forgive and stay awake in the present. Warriors seldom strive alone, and this is true of spiritual warriors as well as military ones. Although each person pursues her own spiritual path and practice, we are fortunate in having communities of support for our practice of compassion. Churches, mosques, synagogues, temples, sanghas, and other religious and spiritual organizations can provide inspiration, encouragement, and structure for practices that help us to follow the path of spiritual and emotional health.

Of course, these organizations can become institutions subject to the flaws of any institution concerned with self-maintenance. In her book, <u>The Dream of God</u>, Verna Dozier writes "...the institutional church, from the resurrection community to the present day, has rejected [Jesus] in favor of something more reasonable, more controlled and more controllable... In other words, I believe Christianity has journeyed far from what Jesus of Nazareth was about."[64] When religious institutions do become preoccupied with control and survival as institutions, they can fall away from compassion and be caught up in the desperate emotions associated with physical survival and power. Then they become the sources for more shame, anger, hatred, and injustice in the world. But when they are able to rise above the temptations of power and remain faithful to their core teachings, they provide structure and support for the kind of focus on justice and compassion that is most healing in our lives.

I have chosen to end this book with a chapter on spirituality because I believe many of us find encouragement in the spiritual literature and practices to which I have referred. We often seek answers to the problems of shame, anger, pain, and loss in communities and practices based on the principles of mindfulness, compassion, justice, and forgiveness. I hope that drawing parallels between these spiritual concepts and practices and those of affect theory, evolutionary psychology, and emotional intelligence will stimulate and support individuals, families, communities, and ultimately societies to move toward realizing these aspirations.

For an individual to gain control over the primal emotional instincts of shame and anger requires much practice, encouragement, and the support of others. To paraphrase a character from Scott Turow's novel, *Ordinary Heroes*, "We are primitive... If we are not to be, we require one another's assistance.

Acknowledgements

I used to think writing was pure fun. That was before I attempted a project of this size. Although I still enjoy the writing process, I have learned how much patience and diligence is required to finish a book. My admiration for all authors has increased immensely, especially those who introduce new ideas or synthesize ideas for the lay reader. I am especially indebted to the writings of Gershen Kaufman and Daniel Goleman, whose work I have cited repeatedly.

I know I could not have come to this page without a great deal of support and encouragement. I would like to acknowledge and thank some of the people who have helped and supported me in bringing this book to completion.

My writing coach, Geoff Michaelson, helped me tremendously in believing that I could complete this project. His gentle and persistent encouragement kept me going until I could see the light at the end of the tunnel. Several patient and thoughtful readers, including: David and Stephanie Deutsch, Bob Ewald, Henry and Mary Lynn Ernstthal, Gene Kendall, and Daniel Venne gave me very useful feedback. John and Joan Kavanaugh were kind enough to spend many hours during our vacation together reading the book and giving me important suggestions. A number of clients whom I cannot name for reasons of confidentiality read drafts of one or more chapters at different stages and told me what was clear and helpful and what was not. The Rev. Paul Abernathy made generous, detailed, and insightful comments on an early draft of the chapter on Shame and Spirituality. Throughout the writing process, many friends have given deeply appreciated encouragement.

The cover, beautifully designed by Stewart Andrews, came as such a delightful surprise that it energized us for the final sprint to publication. Aimee Bennett formatted the final manuscript to make the interior consistent and readable.

Finally, my last and best editor, my wife, Penny, labored patiently and painstakingly to polish the final product, offering curiosity, creativity, and criticism in keeping with the best advice this book has to offer. Her insights and enthusiasm for the details at the end of the writing process have made it a much better book.

I want to thank in advance any readers who are willing to offer constructive criticism and perhaps even share personal stories of their own that might prove instructive in future explorations of shame and anger and the art of giving and receiving criticism.

Bibliography

Andreas, Steve and Connirae Andreas. Heart of the Mind. Moab UT: Real People Press, 1989.

Armstrong, Karen. A History of God. New York: Ballantine Books, 1994.

Bass, Ellen and Laura Davis. The Courage to Heal. New York: Harper Collins, 1988.

Blanchard, Kenneth H. and Spencer Johnson. The One Minute Manager. New York: William Morrow and Co. Inc., 1981.

Benson, Herbert. The Relaxation Response. New York: Harpertorch, 2000.

Boerboom, Rose Mary. Self-Mastery Workshop: Domestic Violence Treatment and Prevention. South Hopkins, MN: Rose Mary Boerboom, 2001.

Borysenko, Joan. Minding the Body, Mending the Mind. New York: Bantam Books, 1987.

Bradshaw, John. Healing the Shame that Binds You. Deerfield Park, FL: Health Communications Inc., 1988.

Campbell, Joseph. The Hero With a Thousand Faces. New York: Pantheon Books, 1949.

Cohen-Posey, Kate. How to Handle Bullies, Teasers, and Other Meanies. Highland City, FL: Rainbow Books, 1995.

Covey, Stephen R. The 7 Habits of Highly Effective People. New York: Simon and Schuster, 1989.

Darwin, Charles. The Expression of Emotion in Man and Animals, Third Edition (Edited by Paul Ekman). New York: Oxford University Press, 1998.

Davidson, Jeff. The Complete Idiot's Guide to Assertiveness. Indianapolis, IN: Alpha Books, 1997.

Diamond, Jared. Guns, Germs, and Steel. New York: W.W. Norton and Company, Inc., 1997.

Dozier, Verna J. The Dream of God: A Call to Return. Boston: Cowley Publications, 1991.

Erikson, Erik H. Childhood and Society. New York: W.W. Norton and Company, Inc., 1964.

Faber, Adele and Elaine Mazlish. How to Talk so Kids Will Listen & Listen so Kids Will Talk. New York: Avon Books, 1980.

Bibliography

Fisher, Roger, William L. Ury, and Bruce Patton. Getting to Yes: Negotiating Agreement Without Giving In. Ontario, Canada: Penguin Books, 1983.

Fried, Suellen and Paula Fried. Bullies and Victims. New York: M. Evans & Co., 1996.

Goleman, Daniel. Emotional Intelligence. New York: Bantam Books, 1995.

Goleman, Daniel. Working with Emotional Intelligence. New York: Bantam Books, 1998.

Goleman, Daniel. Destructive Emotions. New York: Bantam Books, 2003.

Kabat-Zinn, Jon. Full Catastrophe Living. New York: Dell Publishing, 1990.

Kaufman, Gershen. The Psychology of Shame: Theory and Treatment of Shame-based Syndromes. New York: Springer Publishing Company, 1989.

Kornfield, Jack. The Art of Forgiveness, Lovingkindness, and Peace. New York: Bantam Books, 2002.

Kubler-Ross, Elisabeth. On Death and Dying. New York: Simon & Schuster, Inc., 1969.

Lerman, Liz, and John Borstel. "Critical Response Process: A Method for Getting Useful Feedback on Anything You Make, from Dance to Dessert." Liz Lerman Dance Exchange, 2003.

MacFarland, Barbara and Tyeis Baker-Baumann. Shame and Body Image. Deefield Park, FL: Health Communications Inc., 1990.

Maurer, Robert. One Small Step Can Change Your Life. New York: Workman Publishing Company, 2004.

McCoy, Elin. What to Do When Kids are Mean to Your Child. Mt. Pleasant, NY: Readers Digest, 1997.

McQuiston, John II. Always We Begin Again: The Benedictine Way of Living. Harrisburg, PA: Morehouse Publishing, 1996.

Milam, James R., and Katherine Ketcham. Under the Influence: A Guide to the Myths and Realities of Alcoholism. New York: Bantam Books, 1983.

Nathanson, Donald. Shame and Pride: Affect, Sex, and the Birth of the Self. New York: W.W. Norton and Company, Inc., 1994.

Novash, Paula. "Making Civility Kids' Stuff," The Washington Post (Style Section). Washington, DC: January 4, 2004.

Bibliography

O'Connor, Richard. <u>Undoing Depression: What Therapy Doesn't Teach You and Medication Can't Give You</u>. New York: Little, Brown and Company, 1997.

Olweus, Dan. <u>Bullies at School</u>. Oxford: Blackwell Publishers, Ltd., 1993.

Paterson, Randy. <u>The Assertiveness Workbook</u>. Oakland, CA: New Harbinger Publications, Inc., 2000.

Peck, M. Scott. <u>A World Waiting to be Born: Civility Rediscovered</u>. New York: Bantam Books, 1993.

Potter-Efron, Ronald and Patricia Potter-Efron. <u>Letting Go of Shame</u>. Center City, MN: Hazelden, 1989.

Ricks, Thomas E. <u>Fiasco: The American Military Adventure in Iraq</u>. New York: Penguin Books, 2006.

Schwartz, James. "Death of an Altruist." <u>Lingua Franca</u>, Volume 10, No. 5, July/August 2000.

Schwartz, Jeffrey. <u>Brain Lock: Free Yourself from Compulsive Behavior</u>. New York: Harper Collins Publishers, Inc., 1996.

Seligman, Martin E. P. <u>Learned Optimism: How You Can Change Your Mind and Your Life</u>. New York: Simon and Schuster, Inc., 1990.

Stephens, Anthony, and John Price. <u>Evolutionary Psychiatry</u>. Philadelphia: Taylor and Francis, Inc., 2000.

Stroebel, Charles F. <u>QR: The Quieting Reflex</u>. New York: Berkley Books, 1967.

The Shame Project of the Center for Pastoral Counseling of Virginia. http://www.pastoralcounseling.com/shameproject.html.

Talbott, Shawn M. <u>The Cortisol Connection</u>. Alameda, CA: Hunter House Publishers, 2002.

Windell, James. <u>6 Steps to an Emotionally Intelligent Teenager: Teaching Social Skills to Your Teen</u>. New York: John Wiley & Sons, Inc., 1999.

Wurtman, Judith and Susan Suffes. <u>The Serotonin Solution</u>. New York: Fawcett Columbine, 1996.

Notes

[1] Gershen Kaufman, The Psychology of Shame: Theory and Treatment of Shame-based Syndromes, (New York, Springer Publishing Company, 1989).

[2] Martin Seligman, Learned Optimism: How You Can Change Your Mind and Your Life, (New York, Simon and Schuster, Inc., 1990), p 82 on rumination and depression and p 89-91 on Cognitive Therapy.

[3] Daniel Goleman, Emotional Intelligence, (New York, Bantam Books, 1995); Goleman, Working with Emotional Intelligence (1998); Goleman, Destructive Emotions (2003).

[4] Richard Rogers and Oscar Hammerstein. "I Whistle a Happy Tune," from the musical The King and I.

[5] Jared Diamond, Guns, Germs, and Steel, (New York, W.W. Norton and Company, Inc., 1997).

[6] Kaufman, p 12.

[7] For a detailed discussion, see Daniel Goleman's Emotional Intelligence, especially Appendices A, B and C and p 10-20 on how the brain grew.

[8] Goleman, Emotional Intelligence, p 4-5.

[9] Goleman, Destructive Emotions, p 16.

[10] Comments by Ben Pratt in the Shame Project of the Center for Pastoral Counseling of Virginia (www.pastoralcounseling.com/shameproject.html).

[11] Charles Darwin, The Expression of Emotion in Man and Animals, (New York, Oxford University Press, 1998), p 319.

[12] Kaufman, p 4.

[13] Kaufman, p 26-27.

[14] John Bradshaw, Healing the Shame that Binds You, (Deerfield Park, FL, Health Communications Inc.,1988)

[15] Kaufman.

[16] Joseph Campbell, The Hero With a Thousand Faces, (New York, Pantheon Books, 1949).

[17] Iain Pears, The Portrait, (New York, Riverhead Books, 2005).

[18] Kaufman.

[19] Erik H. Erikson, Childhood and Society, (New York, W.W. Norton and Company, Inc., 1964).

[20] The Shame Project of the Center for Pastoral Counseling of Virginia.

[21] The Diagnostic and Statistical Manual of Mental Disorders, Fourth Edition, (Washington, DC, American Psychiatric Association, 1994).

[22] Anthony Stephens and John Price, Evolutionary Psychiatry, (Philadelphia, Taylor and Francis, Inc., 2000), p 70-71.

[23] Charles F. Stroebel, QR: The Quieting Reflex, (New York, Berkley Books, 1967).

[24] Goleman, Emotional Intelligence.

[25] Jon Kabat-Zinn, Full Catastrophe Living, (New York, Dell Publishing, 1990).

[26] Joan Borysenko, Minding the Body, Mending the Mind, (New York, Bantam Books, 1987).

[27] Judith Wurtman and Susan Suffes, The Serotonin Solution, (New York, Fawcett Columbine, 1996).

[28] Richard O'Connor, Undoing Depression: What Therapy Doesn't Teach You and Medication Can't Give You, (New York, Little, Brown and Company, 1997).

[29] Shawn M. Talbott, The Cortisol Connection, (Alameda, CA, Hunter House Publishers, 2002).

[30] O'Connor.

[31] Stroebel.

[32] Robert Maurer, One Small Step Can Change Your Life, (New York, Workman Publishing Company, 2004).

[33] Goleman, Destructive Emotions, p 17-18.

[34] Rose Mary Boerboom, Self-Mastery Workshop: Domestic Violence Treatment and Prevention, (South Hopkins, MN, Boerboom, 2001).

[35] During EMDR the client attends to past and present experiences in brief sequential doses while simultaneously focusing on an external stimulus. Then the client is instructed to let new material become the focus of the next set of dual attention. This sequence of dual attention and personal association is repeated many times in the session. (from a brief description of EMDR found on www.EMDR.com)

[36] Herbert Benson, The Relaxation Response, (New York, Harpertorch, 2000).

[37] For a brief description of neurofeedback and a collection of articles describing results with neurofeedback, see www.eegspectrum.com.

[38] Stephen R. Covey, The 7 Habits of Highly Effective People, (New York, Simon and Schuster, 1989), p 106-109.

[39] Jeffrey Schwartz, Brain Lock: Free Yourself from Compulsive Behavior, (New York, Harper Collins Publishers, Inc., 1996).

[40] A brief prototype of this protocol can be found in The Heart of the Mind, by Steve and Connirae Andreas, (Moab UT, Real People Press, 1989).

[41] Eriksonian Hypnosis and Neuro-Linguistic Programming through the American Hypnosis Training Academy in Silver Spring, MD.

[42] Kenneth H. Blanchard and Spencer Johnson, The One Minute Manager, (New York, William Morrow and Co., Inc., 1981).

[43] Liz Lerman and John Borstel, "Critical Response Process: A Method for Getting Useful Feedback on Anything You Make, from Dance to Dessert," (Liz Lerman Dance Exchange, 2003)

[44] Roger Fisher, William L. Ury, and Bruce Patton, Getting to Yes: Negotiating Agreement Without Giving In, (Ontario, Canada, Penguin Books, 1983).

[45] Randy Paterson, The Assertiveness Workbook, (Oakland, CA, New Harbinger Publications, Inc., 2000).

[46] Jeff Davidson, The Complete Idiot's Guide to Assertiveness, Indianapolis, IN, Alpha Books, 1997).

[47] Kaufman, p 30.

[48] Paula Novash, "Making Civility Kids' Stuff," (Washington Post Style Section, January 5, 2000).

[49] Adele Faber and Elaine Mazlish, How to Talk so Kids Will Listen & Listen so Kids Will Talk, (New York, Avon Books, 1980), p 100-135.

[50] Faber and Mazlish, p 100-135.

[51] Frank McCourt, Angela's Ashes, (New York, Scribner, 1996).

[52] Elisabeth Kubler-Ross, On Death and Dying, (New York, Simon & Schuster, Inc., 1969).

[53] James R. Milam and Katherine Ketcham, Under the Influence: A Guide to the Myths and Realities of Alcoholism, (New York, Bantam Books, 1983).

[54] Jack Kornfield, The Art of Forgiveness, Lovingkindness, and Peace, (New York, Bantam Books, 2002), p 42.

[55] Jung Chang, The Wild Swans, (New York, Simon and Schuster, 1991).

[56] A description of the PATHS program is available at http://modelprograms.samhsa.gov/pdfs/Details/PATHS.pdf.

[57] Goleman, Destructive Emotions, p 256.

[58] M. Scott Peck, A World Waiting to be Born: Civility Rediscovered, (New York, Bantam Books, 1993).

[59] Diamond.

[60] Thomas E. Ricks, Fiasco: The American Military Adventure in Iraq, (New York, Penguin Books, 2006).

[61] Karen Armstrong, A History of God, (New York, Ballantine Books, 1994).

[62] John McQuiston, II, Always We Begin Again, The Benedictine Way of Living, (Harrisburg, PA, Morehouse Publishing, 1996), p 17.

[63] For a brief synopsis of the work of George Price, the game theorist who added substantially to the theory of "nepotistic altruism" as a group survival strategy, see James Schwartz, "Death of an Altruist," Lingua Franca, (Volume 10, No. 5, July/August 2000).

[64] Verna J. Dozier, The Dream of God: A Call to Return, (Boston, Cowley Publications, 1991), p 3.